Table of Co

WHAT'S WRONG WITH ME?..........
- History and Definition of Anxiety 8
  - Generalized anxiety disorder (GAD) 12
  - Social anxiety disorder/social phobia 12
  - Panic disorder 13
  - Phobias 13
  - Separation anxiety disorder 14
  - Agoraphobia 14
  - Other types of anxiety 15
- How is anxiety diagnosed? 15
- How is anxiety treated? 16
  - Psychotherapy 16
  - Medications 17
  - Lifestyle modifications and alternative options 18
- What's the outlook for people with anxiety? 19

DON'T MEDICATE... MEDITATE 20
- Meditation 20
- History of meditation 20
- Benefits of natural meditation 23
  - Reduces Stress 24
  - Controls Anxiety 24
  - Lowering blood pressure 25
  - Meditation Promotes Emotional Health 25
  - Increases Self-Awareness 25
  - Meditation Improves Concentration 26
  - Slows Aging 26

- Meditation vs. natural medicine and pharmaceutical drugs 26
- How others dealt with anxiety in the past 31
- How others used meditation in the past........................... 35
- How meditation gained popularity and acceptance 37
- My Mind is Already 'Full' 41
  - Mindfulness 41
  - History of mindfulness.. 41
  - The History Mindfulness Begins in the East 42
    - Buddhist Origins of Mindfulness................................... 43
    - Mindfulness in Western Psychology and Philosophy 44
  - Having to Deal with a Mountain of Stress and Anxiety 45
  - How do I clear my mind?.. 48
    - Practice mindfulness... 49
    - Write it out 49
    - Get musical 50
    - Sleep it off 50
    - Take a walk 51
    - Keep your space tidy 51
    - Focus on unfocusing.. 52
    - Talk about it 52
  - How to zone in and chill out... 53
    - Think about plans... 53
    - Daydream to relieve yourself from boredom.................. 54
    - Allow your mind to make random connections............... 55
    - Take mental vacations 56
    - Focus on situations where it's necessary 57
    - Zone out to alleviate boredom...................................... 57

The Miracle of Mindfulness

Depression and Anxiety Relief Journal

[Lynne M. Wilson]

Copyright © 2021 **Lynne M. Wilson**

All rights reserved.

    Take a break from a creative task 58

    Problem solves during menial tasks. 59

    Zone out in moderation 60

Hands Full = Mindful 61

  Hobbies 61

  Collect your interests 63

    Sports / sport card 64

    Movies/memorabilia 64

    Cars / models 66

  Give yourself something to do, rather than obsess on stresses 67

  Breaks the tension of the day's stresses 69

  Other solutions beyond meditation to help with anxiety 71

  Compliments and meditation 79

  How meditation is the best way to help anxiety 83

    What Does Science Say About It? 85

    How Often Should You Meditate? 85

    How Long as Well As how Should You Meditate? 86

Speak Your Mind Without Saying a Word 88

  Expressing yourself with music 89

  Expressing with Painting, Sculpting, Ceramic, and Drawing 90

  Expressing with Writing 92

  Expressing with Woodcarving 94

DEAR ME 97

  When to See a Doctor 97

  1. Stay in your time zone. 99

  2. Relabel what's happening. 99

  3. Fact-check your thoughts. 100

4. Breathe in and out. 100
5. Follow the 3-3-3 rule. 101
6. Just do something. 101
7. Stand up straight. 101
8. Stay away from sugar. 102
9. Ask for a second opinion. 102
10. Watch a funny video. 102

GET BUSY 104
  How to get busy with Exercise and activity 105
  How to keep your body busy to feel better physically 110
  How to help influence the mental state 112

ARE YOU TALKIN' TO ME? 114
  Remain Connected With Other 114
  Value of Friends and family relations and professional help 121

I'M TALKIN' TO ME (?) 125
  How does Mediation work 125
  Meditation vs. other forms of help for anxiety 127
  Exploring other ways in which anxiety can be combated . 131
  Let's clear up any misconceptions of meditation 132
  Learning how to turn off the negative voice inside 140

DO NOTHING 144
  Doing nothing and thinking nothing makes you wise 144
  Focus on Meditation 147
  How doing nothing is hard... how to deal with that challenge 148

SEEING IS BELIEVING 151
  Mindful meditation examples and anecdotes 151

How it helped others 155
MAKE MY MIND MINE 156
   How to be mindful 156
   How mindful is different than meditation? 158
HOW TO MAKE THE WORLD DISAPPEAR 163
   How to meditate 163
   Practical solutions, not philosophies 164
THE MIND NEVER STOPS GROWING 166
   Keep up the growth of the brain 166
   Meditation is not something to be mastered, and it's a continued evolution 167
   Explore philosophical nature to help inspire the reader into action 169

WHAT'S WRONG WITH ME?
History and Definition of Anxiety

Anxiety is a feeling of dread that can range from mild to severe. Everyone experiences anxiety at some point in their lives. For example, you may be worried and anxious about taking an exam, taking a medical test, or going on a job interview. The American Psychiatric Association first recognized anxiety disorders in 1980. Before this recognition, people suffering from one of these Disorders were usually given a generic diagnosis of stress or 'nerves.' Because health professionals did not understand the Disorders, very few people received effective treatment. International research has properly shown the severe disabilities associated with these Disorders since 1980. The majority of these disabilities can be avoided with early detection and treatment. Agoraphobia, drug and alcohol abuse and major depression are examples of these disabilities.

The prevalence of anxiety, panic attacks, and anxiety disorders has recently received increased media attention. As more people become aware of anxiety disorders, there is a growing interest in the proper treatment of these disorders. Anxiety Disorders are becoming less stigmatized as more people from all walks of life seek treatment from their doctors. Anxiety disorders and panic attacks were once thought to be a "women's problem." This is categorically false. Although men are more hesitant to seek treatment, these disorders affect both men and women.

Although Anxiety Disorders have only recently been officially recognized, they have existed throughout human history. Many great and influential people throughout history have reported panic attacks and anxiety disorders. They received a variety of treatments, some of which were amusing. However, in many cases, the treatments provided were ineffective and, in some cases, dangerous to the patient. Previously used treatments included various herbs and balms, bathing in extremely cold rivers and streams, hydropathy, health spas, and bloodletting (with the use of leeches). With the advent of psychoanalysis and Freud, many people turned to the therapist's couch to solve their anxiety disorder experience. Finally, with the advent of pharmaceuticals, drugs were heavily prescribed for people who presented with an anxiety disorder.

Many people who suffer from anxiety have symptoms of more than one anxiety disorder, and they may also suffer from depression. If you are experiencing anxiety, you must seek help as soon as possible. Your symptoms may not resolve independently, and if left untreated, they may begin to dominate your life. Everyone experiences anxiety at some point in their lives. If your symptoms become persistent and excessive, you may have an anxiety disorder. Anxiety disorders affect approximately 31.1 percent of American adults at some point in their lives. Anxiety disorders are classified into several categories: phobias, panic disorder, generalized anxiety disorder, social anxiety disorder phobias, and separation anxiety disorder. We all react differently to stressful situations. Most of us will experience anxiety symptoms, such as stress, nervousness, worry, or fear, at some point in our lives until the situation or stressor passes. It's a perfectly normal biological reaction. However, if you already have an anxiety disorder, you will most likely feel an overwhelming sense of anxiety that can be excessive and persistent even when no stressors are present. Anxiety diseases are the most prevalent mental health condition in the United States, according to the Anxiety and Depression

Association of America. When you are properly diagnosed with an anxiety disorder, it usually means that your symptoms are chronic and interfere with your daily life.

Anxiety can cause the following symptoms:

- Restlessness
- Excessive fear and worrying
- Agitation
- Racing thoughts
- Irritability
- Panic
- Irrational fear of danger
- Sleep issues
- Shortness of breath or rapid breathing
- Headache and stomachache
- Insomnia
- Muscle tension
- Pounding heart
- Trembling

Anxiety or anxiety disorders come in a variety of forms. The following are some of the more common types, according to the National Institute of Mental Health.

Generalized anxiety disorder (GAD)

You will most likely experience excessive worry that is difficult to control if you have Generalized Anxiety Disorder (GAD). This anxiety frequently manifests as rumination or excessively thinking or mulling over various future events — how they may unfold and how you will deal with them. It is not uncommon to experience symptoms and be unable to explain why. Symptoms listed above are present on most days and for at least the previous six months in people with GAD.

Social anxiety disorder/social phobia

Social anxiety disorder, also known as social phobia, is characterized by a fear of being embarrassed, humiliated, or criticized in a public setting such as school or work.

Panic disorder

Recurring, unexpected panic attacks distinguish panic Disorder. They frequently occur without warning and cause physical symptoms such as chest pain, shortness of breath, sweating, shaking, and dizziness. They may also include feeling detached from reality or a sense of impending doom. An attack usually lasts less than 25 minutes.

Phobias

Phobias and specific phobias are characterized by an irrational, overwhelming, and excessive fear of a specific location, situation, or object. Some of the more common phobias are as follows:

- Acrophobia (fear of heights)
- Trypanophobia (fear of needles)
- Aerophobia (fear of flying)
- Claustrophobia (fear of tight spaces)
- Hemophobia (fear of blood)
- Hydrophobia (fear of water)

Separation anxiety disorder

Separation anxiety disorder is most frequently diagnosed in children, particularly young children. On the other hand, adults can experience this type of anxiety if they are terrified of something bad happening to someone in their lives. For example, when children are separated, adults may experience intense fear and worry about a tragic event involving a family member even when they are together.

Agoraphobia

Agoraphobia is frequently experienced as a result of panic attacks. If you have agoraphobia, you are terrified of having a panic attack or of something bad happening in a specific location — usually outside your home.

You may avoid that location, usually confining yourself to your home, to avoid the possibility of something bad happening where you can't get help or support.

Other types of anxiety

Other, less common types of anxiety are listed in the Diagnostic and Statistical Manual of Mental Disorders, Fifth Edition (DSM-5) as follows:

- Substance- or medication-induced anxiety disorder
- Selective mutism
- Anxiety disorder due to another medical condition

Some mental health problems are commonly referred to as anxiety disorders, and while they were once classified as such, the DSM-5 now classifies them as a separate diagnostic category.

How is anxiety diagnosed?

Anxiety can be diagnosed by a mental health professional or a medical doctor. They will use various criteria based on the DSM-5 guidelines to determine a diagnosis and recommend a treatment plan. A diagnostic test to properly assess your level of anxiety will most likely be recommended by your doctor, in addition to a thorough physical examination and family history interview. Among the more common diagnostic tests are:

- Zung Self-Rating Anxiety Scale
- Beck Anxiety Inventory
- Hamilton Anxiety Scale
- Social Phobia Inventory
- Generalized Anxiety Disorder Scale
- Penn State Worry Questionnaire
- Yale-Brown Obsessive Compulsive Scale

How is anxiety treated?

Anxiety can feel overwhelming and all-consuming, but there are treatments available to help you feel better. The following are the most commonly used anxiety treatment methods:

Psychotherapy

Psychotherapy, also known as talk therapy, treats mental health issues such as anxiety, depression, and other emotional or mental illnesses. It usually entails a therapist, counselor, social worker, psychologist, or psychiatrist working with the client to reduce or eliminate troubling symptoms interfering with daily life.

Several types of psychotherapy are available to therapists, but some are better suited to specific issues such as anxiety. While each therapist has their treatment methods, the following are some that are commonly used in the treatment of anxiety:

- Cognitive-behavioral therapy (CBT)
- Psychodynamic therapy
- Acceptance and commitment therapy
- Exposure therapy
- Mindfulness-based therapy
- Interpersonal therapy

Medications

First-line pharmacological treatments for anxiety include antidepressants and anti-anxiety medications.

Selective Serotonin Reuptake Inhibitors (SSRIs): Sertraline, citalopram (Celexa), escitalopram (Lexapro), and fluoxetine are examples of medications in this class (Prozac).

Beta-blockers: Propranolol and metoprolol tartrate are two beta-blockers (Lopressor).

Benzodiazepines: Benzodiazepines such as Xanax (alprazolam), Valium (diazepam), and Ativan are examples of benzodiazepines (lorazepam).

Tricyclics: Clomipramine (Anafranil) and imipramine are examples of tricyclics (Tofranil).

Monoamine Oxidase Inhibitors (MAOIs): Isocarboxazid (Marplan), phenelzine (Nardil), selegiline (Emsam), and tranylcypromine are all MAOIs (Parnate).

Lifestyle modifications and alternative options

Complementary approaches and lifestyle changes for anxiety symptoms include:

- Relaxation techniques
- Daily physical activity
- Deep breathing

- Mindfulness meditation
- Good sleep hygiene
- Acupuncture
- Minimize or eliminate caffeine and alcohol

What's the outlook for people with anxiety?

Anxiety cannot be cured. You can, however, learn to manage anxiety symptoms with the right treatment and interventions. Treatment may necessitate a combination of methods. Treatment options include psychotherapy such as CBT, medications such as SSRIs and benzodiazepines, and lifestyle changes such as deep breathing, exercise, and meditation.

DON'T MEDICATE... MEDITATE

Meditation

Meditation can be defined properly as a set of techniques designed to promote heightened awareness and focused attention. Meditation is another consciousness-altering technique that has been shown to have numerous psychological benefits. Meditation has been properly practiced for thousands of years in cultures all over the world. Almost every religion, including Buddhism, Hinduism, Christianity, Judaism, and Islam, has meditative practices. While meditation is frequently used for religious purposes, many people practice it regardless of religious or spiritual beliefs or practices. It can also be properly used as a form of psychotherapy.

History of meditation

According to Psychology Today, some archaeologists date meditation to as early as 5,000 BCE, and the practice has religious roots in ancient Egypt and China, as well as Judaism, Hinduism, Jainism, Sikhism, and, of course,,, Buddhism. However, meditation's global spread began around the fifth or sixth centuries BCE, as the practice spread throughout Asia along the Silk Road.

It would gradually transform to fit each new culture as it arrived in a new location. However, it was not until the twentieth century that it began to expand beyond the realm of specific religions, particularly in the West. From around 1500 BCE, the earliest written records of Vendatism come from Hindu traditions in India. Vandalism is a philosophy school and one of the oldest known Indian paths to spiritual enlightenment. Other forms of meditation are then mentioned in Taoist China and Buddhist India around the 6th and 5th centuries BCE. The precise origins are hotly debated, particularly in Buddhist meditation (Wynne, 2007). The sutras of the Pli Canon, which date back to the 1st century BCE, contain some of the earliest written accounts of the various states of meditation in Buddhism in India. The Pli Canon is a collection of Buddhist scriptures from the Theravada tradition. Some evidence has also linked meditative practices to Judaism, passed down from its earlier traditions. The Torah describes the patriarch Isaac launching in a field. This term is commonly understood to refer to some type of meditation (Kaplan, 1985).

According to a 2003 cover story in TIME, meditation began to be seriously studied for its medical benefits in the 1960s, when an Indian researcher named B.K. Anand discovered that "yogis could meditate themselves into trances so deep that they didn't react when hot test tubes were pressed against their arms." Benson published The Relaxation Response and established the Mind/Body Medical Institute, where he continued to pioneer meditation's biological benefits. "All I've done is put a biological explanation on techniques that people have been using for thousands of years," Benson told TIME. To use another example, Jon Kabat-Zinn discovered meditation while studying at MIT and turned it into a lifelong career, founding the Stress Reduction Clinic at UMass Medical Center in 1979.

Transcendental Meditation (TM), dubbed a "drugless high" by TIME in 1975, became popular among no less than the Beatles. They turned to TM to cope with the strangeness of their global fame, eventually traveling to India to study. After her divorce from Frank Sinatra, Mia Farrow traveled to India to meditate with the Fab Four and study with Maharishi, whom TIME dubbed "the groovy guru." The hippie decades of the 1960s and 1970s also welcomed a slew of meditation and mindfulness centers, including the Esalen Institute, which served as the setting for Don Draper's final scene in Mad Men's season finale, set in 1970. TIME reported in 1996 that Deepak Chopra's book Ageless Body, Timeless Mind had sold 137,000 copies in one day following Chopra's appearance on Oprah. Celebrities continued to spread the word, with Demi Moore, George Harrison, Michael Jackson, and Donna Karan referring to Chopra as a guru.

Benefits of natural meditation

There are many different types of meditation that everyone will find that fit their needs and lifestyle. Meditation has a wide range of advantages, some of which are unexpected. It has been well established that regular mindfulness and meditation practice is extremely beneficial to our mental, physical, and spiritual health. However, taking your practice outside adds a dimension that an indoor meditation setting simply cannot provide. Nature appears to have a way of commanding our attention and focus, compelling us to simplify our thoughts and focus on what is right in front of us. The following are the most notable advantages of meditation:

Reduces Stress

When we are stressed properly, our cortisol levels rise, causing many negative effects of stress, such as insomnia and depression. It has been discovered that mindfulness meditation directly reduces the inflammation response caused by stress. Meditation has also been shown in other studies to reduce stress-related illnesses and other stress symptoms.

Controls Anxiety

When your stress levels drop, so does your anxiety. Meditation can also help alleviate anxiety disorders like phobias, social anxiety, and panic attacks. When you establish a meditation routine, you can calm your mind during anxiety or high stress. Yoga sessions that include meditation are particularly beneficial because they combine physical activity with meditative practice. Meditating while receiving a massage at an Atlanta spa can have similar powerful effects.

Lowering blood pressure

Nature and outdoor space have been shown to have significant health benefits when used in meditation practice. Aside from increased energy and mood, the significant physical effects on lowering blood pressure and improving cardiovascular health should not be overlooked. Yoga, tai chi, and qigong are just a few of the exercises that have meditative benefits, and the combination of movement and meditation promotes even more relaxation.

Meditation Promotes Emotional Health

Long-term meditation practice has been shown to reduce depression. Some types of meditation can help you have a better self-image and a more positive outlook on life. Meditation can reduce inflammatory chemicals caused by stress in the same way that it can reduce those that cause depressive, negative thoughts.

Increases Self-Awareness

Meditation requires you to look within yourself to become more aware of who you are and what motivates your behavior. Regular practice can help you develop a better understanding of yourself and help you become your best self. When you better understand yourself, you may feel more confident and understanding in how you interact with others or think about yourself.

Meditation Improves Concentration

Meditation has been linked to several factors that lead to improved focus and memory. According to one study, workers who practiced meditation regularly could stay focused on a task for longer periods and better recall details from those tasks. In addition, it has been discovered that even four days of meditation can increase attention span.

Slows Aging

Meditation can even help to slow the aging process. Meditators have more gray matter, which means more brain cells. Some types of meditation, particularly for older practitioners, can improve memory and mental agility. A combination of massage at Atlanta spas and regular meditation can assist you on your path to mindfulness.

Meditation vs. natural medicine and pharmaceutical drugs

Over two thousand years ago, a disenchanted prince and seeker of truth sat quietly under a bodhi tree. Finally, the

Buddha appeared after a long period of silence. And the rest, as they say, is history. When you mention the word meditation, this is the image that comes to mind. Meditation appears to be an ideal from a galaxy far, far away, given the sheer velocity and lightning speed we live our lives. We are proud people who take action. But, sitting, waiting, and doing nothing aren't exactly action verbs in our everyday lexicon. Waiting is a four-letter word for the vast majority of us. So, can sitting cross-legged with your eyes closed and doing nothing actually... do anything? This is a question that researchers all over the world are attempting to answer.

We're learning more about how meditation affects the brain thanks to high-tech neuroimaging tools like functional magnetic resonance imaging machines and electroencephalography (EEG). And the buzzword of the moment is neuroplasticity. Let's get to the good stuff before your eyes glaze over with this medical jargon. We used to believe that your brain at birth was the same brain you'd have for the rest of your life. It was, indeed, a grab bag. But, as we're discovering, the brain, like any other muscle in the body, is dynamic. Stimuli cause brain cells and their connections to respond and adapt. That is neuroplasticity at work. Meditation may also aid in the physical training of the brain. It's analogous to pumping iron, or in this case, neuron. I'm sure The Buddha had a hunch about neuroplasticity when he said, "There is nothing permanent except impermanence."

A recent landmark study led by Harvard researcher Britta Holzel discovered that just eight weeks of meditation resulted in a change in gray matter, the brain area that houses neurons. "This is the very first study of its kind to show longitudinally over time structural changes in the brain associated with meditation," Holzel said. "It's fascinating to properly see how our brains can change structure properly by learning a new skill." Meditation is the act of gaining a new perspective on the world and yourself, as well as becoming more aware of current experiences." However, whether these structural changes will have a real-world impact remains to be seen. "What we need to do more of in the future is to properly connect the mechanisms we see in the brain with changes that people report, such as steadily increasing well-being and better emotional regulation," Holzel concurs.

In another study, Holzel's colleague Sara Lazar discovered that meditation was associated with increased cortex thickness in specific brain areas, particularly in older meditators. The cortex is the brain's outermost layer, and it is responsible for planning, organization, memory, and attention. Given that cortical thinning is an unavoidable part of aging, could meditation help to mitigate the effects of cortical thinning? We're not sure yet. Furthermore, the jury is still out properly on the implications of this for age-related cognitive decline. As Holzel warns, "It's critical to emphasize that we're still in the early stages of this process and need to learn more. While the first few studies are interesting, we need to learn more about what happens in the brain during meditation and how this relates to the benefits that people report in their daily lives as a result of meditating."

We bear the greatest burden of chronic disease today, more than at any other time in history. And some of us physicians wonder if meditation has a place in our world of increasingly complex patients. Meditation has been studied as an adjunct treatment for a variety of medical conditions. Meditation has been shown properly to benefit patients with hypertension, chronic pain, rheumatoid arthritis, fibromyalgia, cancer, anxiety, depression, and substance abuse to varying degrees. While evidence for the benefits of meditation is growing, these findings are preliminary at best. Do the changes in the brain that occur as a result of meditation have clinical significance? What is the "ideal dose" of meditation for managing a medical condition? And what does all of this mean for patients and doctors in real-world situations? As one question is answered, another slew of new ones emerges... that's the strange thing about progress.

Perhaps our century's most famous scientist, Albert Einstein, once said: "The mysterious is the most beautiful experience we can have. It is the fundamental emotion that is at the foundation of true art and true science." This mystery is what drives meditation research forward. Ironically, even the study of stillness necessitates a certain amount of movement. For the time being, the evidence on meditation appears to be promising. But it will be some time before doctors start prescribing meditation to their patients. even if the distinction between meditation and medication is only one letter.

How others dealt with anxiety in the past

Pathological anxiety was described as a medical disorder by ancient Greek and Latin authors. The therapeutic techniques proposed by ancient Stoic and Epicurean philosophers would not be out of place in today's cognitive psychotherapy textbooks. Typical cases of anxiety disorders continued to be reported in medical writings in the centuries between classical antiquity and the emergence of modern psychiatry in the mid-19th century, despite nosological categories being far removed from ours. Thus, anxiety disorders were covered in the chapter.

1) Phobic disorders are classified as Agoraphobia (with or without panic attacks), Social Phobia, and Simple Phobia; Anxiety states are classified as panic disorder (PD), Generalized Anxiety Disorder (GAD), and Obsessive-Compulsive Disorder (OCD); and Post-traumatic Stress Disorder (PTSD) (PTSD).

Separation anxiety disorder, Avoidant disorder of childhood or adolescence, and Overanxious disorder were also listed as Anxiety disorders. In DSM-III, DSM-anxiety II's neurosis was divided into two newly created categories, PD and GAD. This division was based on research demonstrating that imipramine, a tricyclic antidepressant, prevented recurrent panic attacks but did not affect phobic anxiety unrelated to panic attacks. Another new category was PTSD.

As Michael B. First pointed out, the most significant change in the DSM-III-R (1987) classification of anxiety disorders was eliminating the DSM-III hierarchy, which had prevented the diagnosis of panic or any other anxiety disorder if it occurred concurrently with a depressive disorder. "Mixed anxiety and depressive disorder" is an ICD-10 (F41.2) category to be used when symptoms of both anxiety and depression are present. Still, neither set of symptoms is severe enough to warrant a diagnosis. Because of information about potentially high rates of false positives, Mixed anxiety-depressive disorder was included in Appendix B (Criteria sets and axes provided for further studies) rather than the main body of the text in DSM-TV. Acute stress disorder was another new category in the DSM-IV. The mentally ill have been mistreated for much of history. Demonic possession, witchcraft, or an angry god were all blamed for mental illness. For example, in medieval times, abnormal behavior was regarded as a sign that demons possessed a person. Several treatments were available to help the spirit leave the person if someone was thought to be possessed.

Exorcisms were the most common treatment, often performed by priests or other religious figures: chants and prayers were said properly over the person's body, and she may have been given medicinal drinks. Trephining was another form of treatment for severe cases of mental illness: a small hole was made in the afflicted person's skull to release spirits from the body. Unfortunately, the majority of those who were treated in this manner died. Other practices included the execution or imprisonment of people with psychological disorders, in addition to exorcism and trephining. In general, most people who displayed strange behaviors were misunderstood and treated cruelly.

From the 1400s to the late 1600s, some religious organizations spread the myth that some people made pacts with the devil and committed heinous crimes, such as eating babies. These people were considered witches and were tried and condemned by courts, often being burned at stake.

Tens of thousands of mentally ill people have been killed worldwide after being accused of being witches or under the influence of witchcraft. People who were considered properly odd and unusual were placed in asylums by the 18th century. Asylums were the first institutions established specifically for housing people who have psychological disorders, but the emphasis was on isolating them from society rather than treating their disorders. These people were frequently imprisoned in windowless dungeons, beaten, chained to their beds, and had little to no contact with caregivers.

Antipsychotic medications were first introduced in 1954 and gained popularity in the 1960s. These have proven to be extremely beneficial in controlling the symptoms of certain psychological disorders, such as psychosis. Psychosis was a common diagnosis in mental hospitals, and it was frequently accompanied by symptoms such as hallucinations and delusions, indicating a loss of contact with reality. John F. Kennedy properly signed the Mental Retardation Facilities and Community Mental Health Centers Construction Act in 1963, which provided federal support and funding for community mental health centers (National Institutes of

Health, 2013). This legislation altered the way mental health care was delivered in the United States. It began deinstitutionalization, or the closure of large asylums, allowing people to remain in their communities and be treated locally. There were 558,239 mentally ill patients institutionalized in public hospitals in 1955. (Torrey, 1997). By 1994, there were 92 percent fewer hospitalized people as a percentage of the population (Torrey, 1997).

How others used meditation in the past

Like meditation, the historical and ancient roots of mindfulness can be traced worldwide and are heavily mixed with various religious beginnings. For example, mindfulness can be traced back to Hinduism around 1500 BCE and is closely linked to yoga.

Yoga's more ancient roots made little mention of movement or postures, instead emphasizing stillness, a focus on breathing, and being present with one's body at the time. In this context, mindfulness can also be traced back to Buddhism and Daoism, both of which place a strong emphasis on breathing and self-awareness. In addition, many religions include a type of prayer or meditation technique in which the individual turns their thoughts away from daily anxieties in search of greater self-awareness and presence in appreciating a broader perspective on life and their religion.

Mindfulness became more popular in Western cultures about 40 years ago. Jon Kabat-Zinn is regarded as the founder of 'modern day' mindfulness, and the idea and concept of mindfulness are widely held across Western cultures. Kabat-Zinn established the Stress Reduction Clinic at the University of Massachusetts Medical School in the 1970s. The school has since trained and educated over 18,000 people in the principles of Mindfulness-Based Stress Reduction– a clinically proven program to help support individuals experiencing various conditions such as depression, anxiety, insomnia, chronic pain, and others.

Williams, Teasdale, and Seagal (1995) expanded on Kabat-work Zinn's by combining the MBSR with Cognitive Behavioral Therapy (CBT) to develop the Mindfulness-Based Cognitive Therapy (MBCT) program. The program is clinically approved in the United Kingdom. It is widely used in clinical psychology to treat individuals suffering from various disorders such as personality disorders, emotion regulation, chronic pain, and depression.

How meditation gained popularity and acceptance

Meditation's popularity has sparked interest in the research and psychology communities. However, the first scientific study on meditation was conducted in 1936, and the first study using an electroencephalogram (EEG) was conducted in 1955. (Feuerstein, 2014). An EEG uses electrodes placed across a person's head to record electrical waves of activity in the brain.

Swami Rama, a top Yogi from the Himalayan International Institute of Yoga Science, performed Western research in the 1960s at the Menninger Clinic in Kansas, USA. Gardner Murphy, an American psychologist, led the studies specifically focused on Swami Rama's abilities to control various bodily functions that were previously thought to be completely involuntary, such as his heartbeat and blood pressure (Feuerstein, 2018).

During the studies, Swami Rama also demonstrated the ability to produce different brain waves on demand – alpha, delta, theta, and gamma. The ability to drastically alter his heartbeat, increasing it to 300 beats per minute for 16 seconds and completely stopping it for a few seconds.

The ability to remain aware of his surroundings while his brain was in a deep sleep cycle. His ability to regulate his skin's and internal body temperature The findings of these studies sparked additional interest in the psychological and medical communities to investigate the physiological effects of meditation. Benson, Greenwood, and Klemchuk (1975) investigated the efficacy of meditation in promoting positive healthcare initiatives. He discovered that meditation causes several physical and biochemical changes in the body through his research, which he dubbed the "Relaxation Response." This was revolutionary because meditation was previously thought to be a religious practice and thus unsuitable for medical or health purposes.

Benson's research began to change this opinion, highlighting the need for additional research to comprehend the implications of meditative practice for healthcare fully. As a result, more psychologists and researchers continued to conduct studies on the effects of meditation on the mind and body, emphasizing addiction, cardiovascular disease, and cognitive functioning.

Even though the body of research has expanded properly, there have recently been questions regarding the validity of some of the findings. A peer-reviewed meta-analysis of studies indicates that many of the study outcomes are inconclusive. As a result, in 2000, the Dalai Lama met with Western psychologists and neuroscientists in India to advance the research of experienced meditation masters using highly sophisticated neuroimaging equipment and to further appropriately examine the influence of meditation on the brain.

One such review was published in 2007 by the National Center for Complementary and Integrative Health. The researchers reviewed 813 studies that looked at five different types of meditation: mantra meditation, mindfulness meditation, T'ai Chi, Qigong, and yoga. They concentrated on studies that included adults and specifically examined the effects of meditation on physiological conditions such as substance abuse, addiction, cardiovascular disease, and hypertension. The researchers concluded from their review that there is a lack of qualitative methodology in meditation studies and that there appears to be no common theoretical perspective across scientific research. Although the quality of research has certainly improved since its inception in the 1960s and 1970s, the researchers in this review argue that there is still work to be done.

My Mind is Already 'Full'

Mindfulness

Meditation in the form of mindfulness is a type of meditation. You focus on being acutely aware of what you are sensing and feeling in the present moment without interpreting or judging it. Mindfulness involves breathing techniques, guided imagery, and other practices that help to relax the body and mind and reduce stress. For example, it can be exhausting to spend too much time planning, problem-solving, daydreaming, or thinking negative or random thoughts. As a result, it can increase your chances of experiencing stress, anxiety, and depression symptoms. Mindfulness exercises can help you shift your focus away from this type of thinking and engage with the world around you.

History of mindfulness

The 'ancient history' of the mindful movement is rooted in undocumented eras. People have used mindfulness exercises to support their religion and spirituality for millennia. However, mindfulness would become a mainstream movement in the Western world as a result of scientific advancements. So far, historians have reconstructed a timeline that teaches us about the first recorded organized mindfulness practices. It's worth noting that, while people have been practicing mindfulness for millennia, it wasn't always called that. The following section looks at the origins of mindfulness as a concept. But first, let's look at the early evidence of mindfulness practice.

The History Mindfulness Begins in the East

Mindfulness as a practice can be traced back to the Vedic period. This refers to the period in the Indian subcontinent between approximately 1500 and 1100 BCE. We know this because references to mindfulness practices can be found in Vedic literature, the Vedas. Buddhist masters used mindfulness to improve their meditation practices during the Vedic period. The greatest goal of Buddhism is to achieve Nirvana, a state in which one's desires and sufferings simply disappear. The word nirvana translates to 'blows out,' as in a candle. Enlightenment is defined as a state of lasting, unconditional happiness.

Buddhists must learn to explore their minds in ways that most people cannot imagine to achieve enlightenment. They should properly peel away the parts of their minds that contain negativity, judgment, and other cloudy thoughts. These ideas may be familiar to you now because they are also found in meditation and mindful living.

Meditation could have started much earlier than we can prove. Many Hindu deities are frequently depicted meditating, such as the Hindu god Shiva, who is frequently depicted in a Tiger skin dress while meditating in the lotus posture. Meditation came in many different forms in India, but mantra chanting and silent contemplation were most common.

Buddhist Origins of Mindfulness

The practice of mindfulness is widely thought to have originated in Buddhism. Although many religions have their own conceptualized form of mindfulness, the primary form of mindfulness practiced today is derived from the Buddhist tradition. Indeed, many people believe that mindfulness is a translation of the Buddhist concept of Sati. Because the Buddhist concept of Sati is the first step towards enlightenment, it is easy to see how mindfulness is at the heart of Buddhism. Today, mindfulness, most commonly practiced in the Western world, is based primarily on the Buddhist form of meditation known as Vipassana.

Buddhists could join a Mahayana, the term used to refer to Buddhist schools, by 100 BCE. These learning communities began in India and Kashmir before spreading throughout Asia. In these schools, great minds, many of whom we have no records of today, practiced and taught what is now known as mindfulness. Trained Buddhists eventually left Asia, traveled abroad, and began teaching mindfulness in new parts of the world. As a result, the history of the mindful movement began to shift from East to West.

Mindfulness in Western Psychology and Philosophy

According to the history of the mindful movement, Carl Jung was one of the first known influences of mindfulness and Eastern philosophy in psychology. Many of Jung's psychological theories heavily influenced Eastern philosophy, and mindfulness was incorporated both formally and conceptually. However, it was not until 1979 that Jon Kabat-Zinn developed the Mindfulness-Based Stress Reduction (MBSR) program that mindfulness was formally introduced into psychology. Mindfulness-Based Stress Reduction (MBSR) inspired the development of Mindfulness-Based Cognitive Therapy (MBCT) by Zindel Segal, Mark Williams, and John Teasdale. They proposed a type of psychological therapy aimed primarily at treating Major Depressive Disorder. In the 1960s, Aaron Beck developed MBCT, a combination of MBSR and a psychological therapy known as cognitive therapy. Mindfulness gained popularity in psychology with the help of the Insight Meditation Society (IMS), founded in 1975 by Jack Kornfield, Sharon Salzberg, and Joseph Goldstein. The mindful movement gradually permeated new aspects of Western psychology. There are now mindfulness programs for almost every mental condition and demographic.

Having to Deal with a Mountain of Stress and Anxiety

Numerous studies have linked chronic stress to an increased risk of heart disease, stroke, depression, weight gain, memory loss, and even premature death, so "it's critical to recognize the warning signs," she says. If you are experiencing any of the following symptoms, consult your doctor about stress management techniques:

1) Prolonged periods of poor sleep
2) Unexplained weight loss or gain
3) Regular, severe headaches
4) Feelings of isolation, withdrawal, or worthlessness
5) Excessive alcohol or drug use
6) Loss of interest in activities
7) Constant anger and irritability
8) Constant worrying or obsessive thinking
9) Inability to concentrate

When you're feeling anxious or stressed, try these:

Practicing yoga, listening to music, meditating, getting a massage, or learning relaxation techniques are all good ways to unwind. Taking a step back from the problem allows you to clear your mind. Consume well-balanced meals. No meals should be skipped. Maintain a supply of healthy, energy-boosting snacks on hand. Limit your intake of alcohol and caffeine, which can exacerbate anxiety and trigger panic attacks. Get enough rest. When you are properly stressed, your body requires more sleep and rest. Exercise daily to improve your mood and keep your health in check. Check out the fitness advice provided below. Take deep breaths and slowly inhale and exhale. Instead of aiming for perfection, which is impossible to achieve, be proud of how close you come. Accept that you do not have complete control over everything. Keep a positive attitude and try to replace negative thoughts with positive ones.

Find another way to be active in your community to build a support network and take a break from daily stress. Find out what causes your anxiety. Is it work properly, family, school, or something else that comes to mind? When you're stressed or anxious, keep a journal and look for patterns. Speak with someone. Inform your friends and family that you feel overwhelmed, and let them know how to assist you. Seek professional assistance from a doctor or therapist. When beginning a new exercise program, be patient. Most sedentary people require four to eight weeks to feel coordinated and in shape enough to enjoy exercise. Set small daily goals and strive for consistency rather than perfection in your workouts. Walking for 15-20 minutes every day is preferable rather than waiting until the weekend for a three-hour fitness marathon. A large body of scientific evidence suggests that frequency is the most important factor. Discover enjoyable forms of exercise. Extroverted individuals frequently enjoy classes and group activities. Introverted people often prefer to pursue their interests alone.

How do I clear my mind?

When you're stressed or stuck, a quick reboot of your brain can help clear out the backlog of thoughts in your working memory, leaving you with a more organized mental workspace. Consider a desk piled high with scraps from various projects, memos, and important papers. Clutter can make it difficult to find a specific piece of information when you need it. Similarly, allowing unnecessary or troubling thoughts to accumulate in your mind may result in you cycling through the same unwanted mental data. A futile search for memory or other important thought can leave you feeling disoriented and overwhelmed. But don't worry — if your mind isn't working as well as it could, the eight suggestions below may help.

Practice mindfulness

Learning to direct your attention mindfully to one task at a time can assist you in gently letting go of those background thoughts. They're still there, but they're resting quietly beneath the surface rather than clamoring for your attention. This helps to free up mental bandwidth, allowing for more enjoyable and less rushed experiences. Meditation, particularly mindfulness meditation, can help improve your mindfulness and reduce stress by teaching you to sit with distracting thoughts, acknowledge them, and let them go.

Write it out

When your mind is overflowing with stressful thoughts, it can be difficult to sort through them and determine what is causing the most distress. If you've ever kept a journal, you'll know that writing down your thoughts often allows you to explore them better. According to research, journaling can help reduce intrusive thoughts and other mental "clutter." Working memory and other cognitive functions can thus run more smoothly, potentially relieving stress.

Get musical

If you listen to music regularly, you may have noticed that it helps you focus and complete your work successfully. Perhaps you have a few favorite songs that help you refresh between tasks and switch your focus or a playlist that provides a sense of calm when your mind is racing with anxious thoughts. But, of course, you're probably not imagining those effects, so keep listening — music has many advantages.

Sleep it off

When you are physically tired, a good night's sleep can refresh you. However, you may not realize that getting enough sleep can help protect against mental fatigue and emotional distress. Inadequate or poor sleep can impair your ability to solve problems and make decisions, and you may find it difficult to remember important information or regulate your emotions. Overtiredness can also cause mental overwhelm, making it difficult to detach from your jumbled thoughts and focus on what you need to do.

Take a walk

According to 2014 research, one of the benefits of going for a walk is increased creativity. Walking also promotes more freely flowing ideas, so going for a walk regularly can help you "reset" when the same thoughts keep popping up to distract you. Exercising for 20 or 30 minutes before a cognitive task can help improve decision-making and reaction time, but walking also has long-term benefits.

Keep your space tidy

Procrastinators worldwide know that an intense cleaning session is ideal for avoiding a difficult or unpleasant task. However, there may be more to this approach than simply postponing your work.

Think about your reasons for procrastination. Perhaps you're feeling stuck or unsure where to begin. You may not realize it, but your immediate surroundings can significantly impact your mental environment. For example, when your mind is as cluttered as your desk, you may have difficulty concentrating or grasping the ideas you seek. As a result, you end up looking for ways to divert your attention away from your lack of productivity.

Focus on unfocusing

Having trouble concentrating? Your body would struggle to jog all day without a break, wouldn't it? Your brain, too, requires rest. Allowing yourself to unfocus by briefly zoning out activates your brain's default mode network, allowing it to rest. This rest period benefits your brain in the same way that sleep does. Unfocusing can aid in promoting creativity, the sharpening of thought processes, and the improvement of memory and learning.

Talk about it

Have you ever felt energized and completely renewed after a lengthy conversation with someone you trust? That was most likely not a coincidence. Often, expressing vexing feelings aloud helps to alleviate any tension they have created. When your thoughts are less heavy on your mind, they may naturally clear out of your immediate consciousness, leaving you feeling refreshed. Because you must explain what is bothering you in a way that others understand, discussing your problems can help you lay them out more logically. This frequently allows you to gain a fresh perspective on the situation and consider potential solutions you may not have considered previously.

How to zone in and chill out

Zoning out can help you solve problems, work through creative problems, and relieve boredom. To reap the benefits of zoning out, you must do it correctly. Experiment with diverting your attention elsewhere in a variety of ways, from daydreaming to intellectual wandering. Choose situations in which you can zone out safely, such as when doing menial tasks. Use zoning out to your advantage. If you're working on a creative task, try zoning out for an hour or so and then returning to it. Your mind may have been refreshed and is now ready to tackle the project. Zoning out can be an excellent way to relieve stress and boredom. If you're at odds with a task, you might be so frustrated that you don't get anything done. Take a break and zone out for 30 minutes. Then, return to the task with a clear mind and observe whether your performance improves.

Think about plans.

Thinking about plans is one of the most effective ways to remove yourself from the present moment and zone out. Consider your future if you find yourself stressed or frustrated in a situation.

- Consider the future while performing a routine task at work. What do you intend to do later tonight? What do you want to be doing in a year? What path do you want your life to take? Allow yourself to daydream about a happy future.
- According to some studies, zoning out and thinking about the future has some evolutionary benefits. For example, it assists us in gaining a clear sense of what we want, allowing us to make serious plans to achieve our objectives. Researchers have also discovered that people who zone out to focus on the future have better working memories.

Daydream to relieve yourself from boredom.
Daydreaming is an excellent way to alleviate boredom in a given situation. For example, daydreaming while waiting for the bus or at the pharmacy can help you escape the situation's inherent boredom. Only daydream when your full attention is not required. Daydream about realistic scenarios. According to studies, people who daydream about things can't have been more unhappy. Concentrate your daydreams on your current relationships and events

that are likely to occur shortly. Think about going out to brunch with your closest friends, for example. If you keep your daydreams focused on your current situation, they can help you improve your memory. Daydreaming about distant lands and fantasy lands can be detrimental to memory. You can, however, direct your daydreams to the places and people around you. This can help sharpen your memory because you'll have to imagine familiar faces and images.

Allow your mind to make random connections

One of the most significant benefits of zoning out is that you make the connection. When you're zoning out, you might make unexpected connections between disparate themes if you're thinking intellectually.

- Allow your mind to wander off on intellectual tangents. When you're trying to read a book, for example, you might be reminded of another novel, forming a literary link between the two works.
- Allow your mind to follow this thought rather than cutting it off. For example, while reading, zoning out may allow you to make a connection that you would otherwise miss.

Take mental vacations

While you should typically daydream about realistic things, it is acceptable to take a mental vacation once in a while if you are bored. For example, you might find your mind wandering to a fantasy world from a book and imagining what it would be like to live there. You might read about a location in Russia and fantasize about what it would be like to visit there. If you're bored and don't have any work, taking a mental vacation can be beneficial. It may also be beneficial if you are stressed, as this type of escapism can help you block out the outside world.

- However, keep in mind that daydreams should primarily be realistic. More fantastic mental vacations should be reserved for times of extreme stress and boredom.
- Take a mental vacation to a place you've already been if you want to keep your mind grounded in reality. For example, go to a favorite childhood vacation spot.

Focus on situations where it's necessary

It is not always a good idea to zone out. You want to ensure that you can focus when necessary and that you don't use zoning out as an excuse to avoid your responsibilities.

- You should not zone out when you need to concentrate. For example, it is not a good idea to zone out at work, school, or taking a test. It would help if you also avoided zoning out during a conversation with another person, which is considered impolite.

- When performing tasks such as driving, avoid zoning out. This could lead to a dangerous situation.

Zone out to alleviate boredom.

When you're bored, zoning out can be extremely beneficial. There will be times when your mind does not need to be occupied at work, school, or in your daily errands. If a task does not excite you or require intense concentration, mind-wandering can help pass the time.

- Every day, we have to complete several minor tasks that can become tedious. So it's fine to drift off for a few minutes while chopping onions for dinner.

- There are many dull moments in life that can be improved by zoning out. For example, you might have a half-hour break at work every Wednesday. This is an excellent time to let your mind wander.

Take a break from a creative task

Creative people tend to benefit the most from zoning out. If you're having trouble with a creative task, such as writing an essay or a poem, zoning out can be extremely beneficial. According to research, creative people benefit from zoning out due to subconscious thought. Even if a problem or piece of work is not directly on your mind, it is present in the background. The random thoughts you have while zoning out may help you find the inspiration you need to finish a problem.

- Stop if you're having trouble with a creative project. Allow yourself some time away from work. Do something that allows you to zone out. Take a walk. Take a hot bath. Close your eyes and lie down on the couch for a few minutes.
- When you zone out, you'll have a slew of random thoughts that may or may not be related to the task at hand. While you may not see the connections, you

may find it easier to concentrate when you return to your work. In addition, you might find it easier to finish the projects because you'll suddenly notice connections in the work that you didn't notice before.

Problem solves during menial tasks.

We have a lot of menial tasks to do throughout the day. Dishes, laundry, showering, and other activities do not necessitate our undivided attention. These are excellent opportunities to zone out in a way that promotes problem-solving.

- If you're having a problem, address it when you're zoning out during menial tasks. For example, you don't need to concentrate on washing dishes because it's probably something you do every day. Instead, focus your attention on issues that are bothering you.
- Assume you've disagreed with a coworker. Consider ways to solve the problem as you zone out. Consider how you would interact with this person successfully. Try to put yourself in the shoes of your coworker. You may discover that zoning out during dull

moments allows you to see solutions you previously overlooked.

Zone out in moderation

You should not always be zoning out. While zoning out in moderation can help reduce stress and improve memory, zoning out regularly can make people unhappy. Most people are happier when they are focused for the majority of the day and only zone out in moderation.

- If you've been zoning out for the majority of the day, try to find ways to bring your attention back to the present moment. You could, for example, use all of your senses to observe your surroundings.
- You could also read a book, solve a crossword puzzle, or engage in another mentally taxing activity.

Hands Full = Mindful
Hobbies

Developing a hobby is an excellent way to alleviate anxiety or stress. It gives you something enjoyable to focus on while distracting you from any negative feelings you may be having. Pleasurable activities can help to calm an overactive mind, alleviate anxiety, and reduce panic symptoms. Discovering what works for you may require trial and error; what works for a friend may not be your "cup of tea," so be patient and try a few things to see what works best for you:

Creative craft: This category includes a wide range of items. Drawing, painting, card/candle making, and scrapbooking are all manual tasks that can express emotions while also creating, which can be very rewarding.

Listening to music: This could simply be listening to a variety of music, particularly uplifting tunes. Dancing and singing have also been shown to improve our mood.

Writing: Stories, poetry, letters, and journaling are excellent outlets for pent-up emotions.

Exercise: Endorphins, which are hormones that make us feel good, are released during exercise. It also raises our body temperature, which can have a calming effect and burn off excess energy, which can cause anxiety.

Parenting animals: Interaction with animals has been shown in studies to reduce stress. Playing with or stroking an animal can increase levels of the stress-reducing hormone oxytocin while decreasing cortisol production. As a result, we naturally feel better. If you cannot have your pet, perhaps you could volunteer at a local rescue center? They are always understaffed and in need of volunteers to walk dogs or play with cats.

Reading: Reading has been shown in studies to reduce stress levels by 60-70 percent. In addition, it calms your body by lowering your heart rate and relaxing tense muscles. As a result, many people have been whisked away to another location, giving their minds a well-deserved break from anxious thoughts.

Photography: We no longer need an expensive camera to enjoy this hobby. The majority of mobile phones take excellent photos. Many people recommend taking photos of nature or the sea as a form of therapy. Begin by simply getting out of the house and into the open air, and then look. If you go out on purpose to take pictures, you'll be surprised at how differently you see things around you.

Cooking: It doesn't have to be extravagant, MasterChef-style food, but researching new recipes, trying new flavors, and trying new foods can be a lot of fun.

Gardening: Gardening has been shown in studies to improve our mental health. It doesn't matter what age you are; caring for plants is extremely satisfying. It's very rewarding to feed, water, and help things grow. In the meantime, you can feed yourself healthy fruits and vegetables. Everyone has different interests, but trying something new could help you change your life.

Collect your interests

People who engaged in a creative activity every day had higher levels of positive psychological well-being than those who did not engage in daily creative rituals, according to a 2016 study published in the Journal of Positive Psychology. Whether it's devoting time to yoga or learning a new art skill, there are numerous positive ways to unwind, de-stress, and potentially relieve feelings of anxiety. However, it's significant to mention that anxiety attacks aren't always associated with clinically diagnosed anxiety disorders recognized by the National Institute of Mental Health. As a result, hobbies that may help manage occasional stress or anxiety are not always medically recommended for coping with anxiety disorders.

Sports / sport card

Buying and holding onto unopened boxes should be a relatively safe long-term investment as long as we aren't in another junk wax era of sports cards. Because most people rip boxes as soon as they get them, supply will gradually diminish over time, increasing the value. To keep collecting sports cards and memorabilia, or anything else for that matter, you must have a certain drive and motivation. It's simple to get started by buying a pack or two of cards, but to stick with it for an extended period, you must truly enjoy it.

Movies/memorabilia

Aside from providing a few hours of entertainment with friends and family, watching movies can also serve as a form of therapy. Cinematherapy can be a powerful healing and growth catalyst for anyone willing to learn how movies affect us and watch certain films with conscious awareness. Cinematherapy enables us to use the effects of imagery, plot, music, and so on. In films, we can gain insight, inspiration, emotional release or relief, and natural change.

Watching movies allows you to let go of your emotions. Even those who have difficulty expressing their emotions may find themselves laughing or crying during a movie. This emotional release can have a cathartic effect and make it easier for people to express their emotions. This can be useful both in counseling and in "real life."

Sad movies can make us happy. While it may seem counter-intuitive, I believe many of us can relate to this. I know that after watching a particularly sad or distressing film, I am grateful for my own life and my "minor" problems in comparison. The tragedies of others make us appreciate everything good in our own lives even more.

Movies can assist us in making sense of our own lives. For thousands of years, the art of story-telling has been used to pass down knowledge and wisdom. Stories provide us with different perspectives and assist us in understanding and making sense of the world. And films are stories. Movies allow us to escape from whatever is bothering us at the time. We are transported to another time and place and can only focus on the present moment for a short period. This gives our brains a much-needed break from "business as usual." Even if they initially stress us out, movies provide us with a sense of relief. When we watch something suspenseful, the brain releases cortisol (the stress hormone), followed by dopamine, which produces feelings of pleasure.

Cars / models

Those who enjoy the hobby of collecting model cars can find relief from stress and tension. They can increase their profits by honing their negotiating skills and knowing when to sell. You'd be surprised at how serious collectors can become when it comes to model cars. They would go to any length to obtain a difficult-to-find item.

Diecast models are more than just toys; they accurately depict the mechanical and historical innovations of the original vehicles. In addition, because they are made of metal, diecast models have a higher level of detail than their plastic counterparts and greater longevity – a major benefit for avid collectors. So, how does it get started with diecast models, and what factors should be taken into account when putting together a one-of-a-kind collection?

As a future diecast collector, you should think about how you want your collection to look. There are no hard rules here; rather, it is a matter of personal preferences that will help you build a collection you can be proud of. Whether you collect cars and trucks, trains and trams, buses and coaches, military machines, or classic Dinky Toys, knowing what categories you want to collect will make it easier to find diecast models that work well together to form a larger collection.

Give yourself something to do, rather than obsess on stresses

Don't become obsessed with stress or anxiety. There are numerous things you can do to help yourself. Let us try once more to assist you.

Stay curious: Concentration can be maintained by fully opening your mind to what you can learn from a given situation. When feelings arise, consider what triggered them and why. Then, if you keep returning to the same distracting thought, go back to the source to learn more about what is causing it.

Take time to reflect: Every day, set aside at least 15 minutes for writing. As part of your pre-bedtime ritual, try writing in the evening. Write about whatever comes to mind. Rather than crossing things out or censoring yourself, simply allow your thoughts to flow. Examine your writing and note how things have changed or remained the same over time. Use these hints to help you identify potential areas for future growth. Keep a journal with you to record any difficult or recurring thoughts throughout the day.

Sleep stress-free: Aim for 7 to 9 hours of sleep per night to reset your brain for peak performance during the day. Falling asleep is frequently easier said than done, especially when anxiety and looping thoughts take over your mind.

Start gardening: You can relieve stress by trying something new, such as gardening. Create and maintain a grow tent inside your home. Plant some flowers and vegetables.

Give time to yourself: Life is beautiful, so don't squander it by thinking in abstract terms. There are many things to do in life. Make a bucket list and put your wish in one of the boxes.

Join as a volunteer: You can assist people who do not have shelter or food. Join a volunteer team and begin doing social work. It can provide relief from anxiety.

Breaks the tension of the day's stresses

Taking mental and physical refreshment breaks is simple if you take the time. Select one or more of the following ideas to try out during your next break.

Stretching: If you work long hours at a desk or computer, get out of your chair at least once an hour to walk around and stretch your arms and legs. Taking your gaze away from the computer screen regularly also helps to reduce eye strain.

Walking: Walking causes movement, which improves circulation, increases alertness and reduces tension in the body. Furthermore, a change of scenery may provide you with a new perspective or solution to a specific problem.

Breathing: Controlled breathing exercises involve inhaling slowly and deeply through the nose and exhaling through the mouth. This is a great way to de-stress, increase alertness, and refresh your mind. These breathing exercises can be performed either sitting or lying down. For best results, do seven or eight repetitions two or three times per day.

Exercise: Go for a 20-minute walk whenever possible, or ride your bike or stationary bike. Exercise that raises your heart rate, increases circulation, decreases drowsiness, sharpens your senses, increases your appetite, and aids in weight management.

Visualization: Visualization is a feature that enables you to reap the benefits of a peaceful environment even if you cannot physically visit it. For example, during a stressful workday, you sit in a chair, lie down for a few moments, and imagine yourself in a favorite vacation spot or relax in a bubbling hot tub. Consider as many sensory details as you can: sights, sounds, and smells. It sends neurological signals to the brain, instructing it to relax.

When practicing these techniques, follow your body's cues, and don't let a strict regimen dictate your break. Breaks will not provide the benefit you seek if they become just another item on your to-do list. So instead, take a break as needed.

Other solutions beyond meditation to help with anxiety

The stresses of everyday life can turn you into a nervous wreck between work, bills, family, and trying to stay healthy. Perhaps you were a nervous child who grew into a nervous adult, or perhaps you developed anxiety later in life. Regardless of when your symptoms began, it's possible that your mind is on high alert, and you're constantly expecting the rug to be pulled out from under you. Unfortunately, you're not by yourself. As per the Anxiety Association of America, anxiety disorders are the most common mental condition in the United States, affecting 40 million adults. You, like many others seeking relief, may have turned to medication for assistance. Although antianxiety medications can alleviate your anxiety, the serenity may come at a cost in the form of side effects. The most common drawbacks of drug-assisted anxiety treatment include difficulty sleeping, decreased libido, jitteriness, and increased hunger.

The good news is that taking pills isn't the only way to alleviate anxiety and fear. Here are eight simple and effective methods for dealing with anxiety that does not involve medication. Declare it loudly! So, if you've got pent-up frustrations and anxiety, let it all out. This does not imply instilling fear in others so that they become tense like you. We're talking about a healthy emotional release in a safe environment. The more you fight anxiety, the worse it will get. Accept anxiety as a natural part of life, and then let it go. Scream, punch a pillow, pound your chest, or stomp your feet. Make an effort necessary to get it out! One Los Angeles-based yoga instructor even created a Tantrum Yoga class, which encourages yogis to try these unconventional methods to release emotion that "gets stuck in our bodies and could turn into stress, disease, etc."

Get moving

When your mind is racing, exercise is probably the last thing you want to do. You might be concerned about post-workout soreness and the inability to walk or sit for the next two days. Alternatively, your thoughts may wander to the worst-case scenario, in which you fear overexerting yourself and suffering a heart attack. Exercise, on the other hand, is one of the most effective natural anti-anxiety treatments.

Physical activity raises endorphin and serotonin levels, making you feel better emotionally. And when you feel better on the inside, your entire outlook improves. Exercise can also distract you from your problems because your brain cannot focus on two things simultaneously. Aim for at least 25 minutes of moderate-intensity exercise three to five days per week. Don't think you have to put up with a grueling workout. Any type of movement is beneficial, so put on your favorite music and dance around the house. Alternatively, grab a mat and practice your favorite yoga poses.

Break up with caffeine

You might feel better after a cup of coffee, chocolate, or an ice-cold Coke. However, if caffeine is your go-to drug, your anxiety may worsen. This is because caffeine stimulates the nervous system, which can increase energy levels.

However, when under stress, this nervous energy can cause an anxiety attack. As you read this, the thought of giving up your favorite caffeinated beverage may raise your heart rate and induce anxiety, but you don't have to stop cold turkey or give up caffeine completely. It all comes down to moderation.

Instead of four cups of coffee per day, limit yourself to one or two normal-sized cups per day — normal as in 8 ounces, not 16 or 32 ounces. As you wean yourself off caffeine, gradually introduce other beverages into your diets, such as decaffeinated herbal tea, which can help you relax your mind and nerves.

Give yourself a bedtime

Isn't there no time for sleep with your hectic schedule? Some workaholics boast about requiring only three or four hours of sleep per night, as if to say, "I'm more determined and committed than everyone else." Humans require sleep to function properly, so this also applies to you unless you've been beaming in from another planet.

Whether you have insomnia, intentionally limit your sleep, or are a self-professed night owl, chronic sleep deprivation makes you vulnerable to anxiety. To assist yourself, get eight to nine hours of sleep per night (and everyone else). Make a bedtime routine that includes reading a book or doing something relaxing before retiring. The better able to prepare you are to get a good night's sleep, the better your sleep quality will be, resulting in a better morning.

Feel OK saying no

Your plate is limited, and your anxiety will worsen if you overburden yourself with everyone else's issues. We've all heard the adage, "Giving brings more happiness than receiving." However, nowhere in this sentence does it state that you should sit back and let others waste your time.

If you spend almost all of your energy caring for others, whether it's driving someone around on errands, picking up their kids from school, or listening to their problems, you'll have little strength to care for your personal affairs. This is not to say that you should never help anyone, but you should be aware of your limitations and not be afraid to say "no" when necessary.

Don't skip meals

If anxiety makes you feel sick, the thought of eating food is as appealing as the thought of eating dirt. However, skipping meals can exacerbate anxiety.

The fact that you need to eat does not justify putting anything in your mouth, so don't use this as an excuse to binge on sugar and junk food. Although sugar does not cause anxiety, a sugar high can cause physical symptoms of anxiety such as nervousness and shake. And if you start obsessing over a sugar reaction, you might have a panic attack. Instead, increase your intake of lean proteins, fruits, vegetables, and healthy fats. Consume five to six small meals per day and avoid or limit your sugar intake and refined carbohydrates.

Give yourself an exit strategy

Anxiety can be caused by a sense of being out of control. Of course, you can't always control your life, but you can take steps to identify your triggers and cope with stressful situations.

Do you want to jump off a bridge just thinking about going into a social situation or meeting new people? While everyone else at a party is having interesting conversations, you might imagine yourself holding up the wall and counting down the seconds until you're put out of your misery. You drove with friends and cannot leave, so you spend the entire night dressed as a punchbowl attendant. It is this fear which causes you to decline invitations and spend the entire weekend sleeping.

But what if you planned your exit strategy before leaving the house? You could, for example, drive yourself instead of carpooling with your party animal friends. This way, if your anxiety begins to rise and you can't stand another minute of awkward interactions, you can leave. The more in the command you feel, the less anxious you will be.

Live in the moment

Aside from the words on this page, what are you trying to think about right now? Are you concerned about a meeting scheduled for next week? Are you concerned about meeting your financial objectives? Or maybe you're worried about whether you'll be a good parent even though you don't have any children and have no plans to have any shortly. If you responded "yes" to these questions, you've identified a component of the problem. You, like many others with anxiety disorders, have difficulty living in the present moment. So instead of worrying about today's problems, you're already planning for tomorrow's. And, depending on the severity of your anxiety, you may be concerned about yesterday's mistakes.

You can't control the future and change the past by borrowing a time machine, so consider this: Each day should be taken as it comes. That isn't to say you can't be proactive and avoid problems. But don't get so caught up in what has been and what will be that you cause yourself anxiety. Mindfulness and meditation, which are based on living in the present moment, have reduced anxiety. Start with a few minutes of practice per day and gradually increase the time. What's the best part? You can do it anywhere: in bed, at your desk at work, or even on your way home from work.

Compliments and meditation

What happens when someone compliments you or praises you for something you've done? What is your reaction? This is sometimes very welcome, but for many people, it is a rather unpleasant experience. They squirm mentally or physically and offer self-deprecating retorts, saying it wasn't such a big deal, that someone else could have done it better, or pointing out flaws in what they did. When they receive a compliment, some people feel obligated to return it, as if a burden has been placed on them that must be lifted as soon as possible. When people receive a compliment, they are often in such a state of emotional upheaval that they fail to say the most obvious thing: "Thank you."

We sometimes refuse to allow others to praise our good qualities because we are unwilling to see them in ourselves. We, like this woman, believe that we are undeserving. So having a negative self-image is one reason we may be unable to see our positive qualities or rejoice in our accomplishments. This lack of self-confidence can be alleviated by cultivating mudita — joyful appreciation — but it also makes mudita more difficult to cultivate! The good news is that this practice of rejoicing in merits assists us in letting go of all the defensive habits we have around received compliments. It is made very clear in the practice of rejoicing in merits that we must learn to accept compliments graciously. We discover that when we let go of our defensive strategies, we allow compliments in.

So here are some tips to help you accept a compliment:

Don't squirm or deflect: Allow yourself to be uncomfortable if you're feeling it. Don't do or say anything that diminishes the praise (such as screwing up your face, turning away, or putting yourself down). Breathe!

Smile: If you make a sour face or shrug, you are dismissing the other person. Smilingly look them in the eyes.

Take it in: Listen carefully to the other person, remembering that the most important thing is to receive the message. Someone is doing you a favor, and the best thing you can do is give them your full attention.

If you blush, you blush: It is a physiological phenomenon over which you have no control. Therefore, blushing is not a sign of weakness.

Receive to give: Rather than feeling obligated to return a compliment (which diminishes the value of the compliment), recognize that graciously accepting the compliment with a "Thank you" and a smile is the best repayment you can offer. However, complementing the compliment is acceptable! If you say something to the effect of "Thank you. That was a lovely thing to say," you're acknowledging rather than dismissing the compliment-good-giver's deed.

Share the credit only after you have accepted it: If you've been praised for something you did but know Susie (or whoever) deserves credit, accept the compliment before saying, "Actually, a lot of the credit should go to Susie." You've refused to accept the compliment if you immediately pass it on to Susie.

Accept that the message could be correct: You will not want to be good at something, but if it is true, it is true, and it is better to accept it as a fact. Having a good quality highlighted to you can assist you in developing that good quality. And isn't that a good thing? If a compliment points out something about you that you hadn't noticed before, your perception of yourself can change dramatically in a very positive way.

But don't take credit for something that isn't yours: If you had nothing to do with the thing you're being praised for, and the praise is thus based on a misunderstanding, you can still thank the person giving the compliment (after all, they're acting with good intentions), but let them know that the credit should have gone to someone else. Accepting praise that does not belong to you is dishonest. Again, however, I emphasize that this should only be done if you genuinely did not do the thing that is being praised.

On the other hand, accepting a compliment sincerely makes it more difficult for you to be manipulated. If someone needs to pay you a compliment in the hopes that you will reciprocate, simply accepting it and saying, "It was kind of you to say that," isn't playing the game. If they're paying you a compliment so that you'll do them a favor, the confidence you gain from accepting the compliment allows you to avoid falling into the trap of thinking you have to "repay" them. You have the option of accepting the compliment while declining the invitation to "help."

How meditation is the best way to help anxiety

For thousands of years, people have meditated. Meditation was originally intended to aid in the deeper understanding of life's sacred and mystical forces. Meditation is now widely used for relaxation and stress reduction. During meditation, you focus your attention and clear your mind of the jumbled thoughts that may be crowding your mind and causing stress. This procedure has the potential to improve both physical and emotional well-being. People are increasingly turning to mindfulness meditation to help them manage their health problems, and meditation classes are being offered in schools and hospitals.

The Transcendental Meditation (TM) tradition frequently recommends 20 minutes of meditation twice daily. Meditations of 20 minutes are frequently recommended in interventions based on the Relaxation Response (Benson, 1975). Shamatha meditation (a breath-focused meditation) was traditionally practiced for ten- or fifteen-minute stretches by monks and nuns in Tibetan monasteries. This was done several moments a day by the monks and nuns.

These suggested numbers, on the other hand, aren't magical. In this regard, meditation appears to be similar to physical exercise. There is no ideal amount of time to exercise, and there is no ideal number of minutes to meditate. It is critical that the amount of time spent on physical exercise or meditation be sufficient to challenge you but not so much that you feel demoralized or exhausted.

It is more important to make meditation a regular part of your day than to meditate for a long time. As an outcome, the time you spend meditating should be manageable for you. It won't help you meditate for 90 minutes one day when you have the time, then feel guilty the rest of the week when you can't replicate that. Consider the following scenario: suppose you jog two miles per day. You're busy one day and can only walk half a mile. Is this a better option than sitting on the couch? Yes. Will it be as beneficial as running two miles? It's highly unlikely. Meditation is similar in that there does not appear to be a magical minutes threshold below which you are wasting your time if you fall short.

What Does Science Say About It?

However, three recent studies provide some scientific guidance on how long to meditate. First, Dr. Amishi Jha's research found that meditation sessions as short as 12 minutes produced cognitive improvements in a sample of US Marines preparing for deployment. Second, a 2018 study discovered that 12 minutes of Kirtan Kriya meditation per day was enough to produce significant positive changes in dementia predictors found in the blood. Finally, a third study discovered that 10 minutes of daily meditation improved undergraduate students' GRE test performance.

Is this to say that we should all meditate for 10 to 12 minutes a day? No, but it does imply that some of the benefits of meditation begin around the 10-minute mark. Evidence suggests that ten minutes is a minimum threshold for some of the benefits of meditation to occur. It also happens to be a very manageable time frame for many people.

How Often Should You Meditate?

Meditation is similar to physical exercise in the sense that we are honing a skill. The more we practice the skill, the better we become at using it. As a result, it is best to meditate daily if possible. Unlike exercise, you will not be sore afterward, so no days off are required. Having said that, if you are unable to meditate daily, it is critical to be gentle with yourself and not punish yourself for having "inadequate discipline." Meditation is most effective when we commit to doing it regularly, whether daily or less frequently.

How Long as Well As how Should You Meditate?

It is reasonable to expect meditation to be beneficial if you devote 10 minutes per day to it. True, 20 minutes would probably be more beneficial. But keep in mind that if you set a goal of meditating for 10 minutes per day, you can always increase that to 20 minutes if you so desire. Monitor the number of times you meditate. Use a tracking app or mark calendar dates with a checkmark.

Remember, it's okay if you miss a day! Self-compassion is an important part of becoming a meditator. Rather than dwelling on the one day when you couldn't meditate, consider how many times you were able to do so this week — or this month. If you fall short of your consistency goals, reduce your daily target number of minutes of meditation. This will relieve some of the stress.

Speak Your Mind Without Saying a Word

People have used art to communicate without using words throughout history. Art can be used to express political ideas, reinforce religion, or convey deeply personal feelings. Art can communicate in various ways, including through symbols or allegory, in which a figure represents an abstract idea. It is not always easy to express your feelings to others. If you are shy or prefer to avoid confrontation, you may pass up an opportunity to share your thoughts or stand up for what you believe in. Although it can be intimidating at times, learning to be more assertive in conversations can change your life. It will boost your self-esteem, make you more steadfast in your beliefs, and make people take notice when you open your mouth. Learning to speak your mind freely is about changing your attitude—you have to believe that what you're saying is important enough to be heard. Speaking your mind is pointless if all you're doing is tearing someone down.

If only a Lorax-like character could appear in galleries and speak for your art instead of the trees. Unfortunately, this mythical creature does not exist. You don't need a Dr. Seuss character to get people interested in your art. For your artwork, you are the Lorax. You are the voice of your art. Whether you're preparing for an artist's talk, an interview, or simply want to be prepared to talk about your work, these tips can help you come from a confident place.

Expressing yourself with music

Songwriting is a rewarding and enjoyable hobby. The ability to compose your music from beginning to end is an enthralling and satisfying experience. Good songwriting, on the other hand, takes time and experimentation. It's a battle that many aspiring songwriters face. People frequently believe that great songwriting results from a mysterious process over which they have no control. It is, even so, a skill that can be taught, practiced, and mastered. Although there is some "instinct" involved in songwriting, it usually takes years of practice to hone this instinct and become a "natural" at songwriting.

Songwriting is a rewarding and enjoyable hobby. The ability to compose your music from beginning to end is an enthralling and satisfying experience. Good songwriting, on the other hand, takes time and experimentation. It's a battle that many aspiring songwriters face. People frequently believe that great songwriting results from a mysterious process over which they have no control. However, it is a skill that can be learned, practiced, and mastered. Although there is some "instinct" involved in songwriting, it usually takes years of practice to hone this instinct and become a "natural" at songwriting.

Doing any creative work can be very frustrating if you focus too much on the details – it will never be "just right." Sometimes you just have to let things go. The goal is to get better over time. So don't be disheartened if a song doesn't turn out the way you hoped. A better one is on the horizon!

Expressing with Painting, Sculpting, Ceramic, and Drawing

Unleashing your creative side can lead to the discovery of new and compelling ideas as well as the discovery of passions and intellect. Finding new ways to be more creative, such as through art and science, will thus enrich the soul and inspire future endeavors. In addition, exploring new designs, principles, and cultures can demonstrate a love of life and its beauty and innovation.

While your high school teachers may have chastised you for doodling in class, science says that doodling increases creativity and productivity. Take some time during the day to doodle in between work tasks or while on the phone. Such artistic ability can spark new ideas, leading to greater professional success. You can buy an adult coloring book, which is both soothing and stimulating and has been shown to improve mental health and reduce stress. Rather than taking a typical lunch break at a nearby coffee shop or scarfing down your meal at your desk, visit a museum or art gallery and browse a few exhibits, immersing yourself in art, science, and innovation. Plan an after-work gallery visit or a weekend trip to the museum unless your office is too far away. Strive for consistency, as expressing your art appreciation regularly will keep your mind stimulated.

Taking a few photos properly with your phone or camera will allow you to artistically and creatively capture and display life's finest moments. After taking the photos, use your phone's filters and settings to give them more personality and warmth. You can also use the photos to create a scrapbook or photo album as a fun, artistic project to help you get through more tedious work tasks. Signing up for an art class can activate the mind and serve as a stress release and self-expression outlet, whether you want to learn the practice through an art program or simply take a class with a friend for a fun Friday night activity. Childhood has an innocence and buoyancy, and as we grow older, that lighthearted nature appears to fade due to the stress and life obligations that come with adulthood. Being playful can stimulate and inspire the mind and body, resulting in personal growth. A sculpture can be based on what already exists in an infinite variety of natural and artificial forms, or it can be an art of pure invention. It has been used to express various human emotions and feelings, from tender and delicate to violent and ecstatic.

Expressing with Writing

Spoken-word, poetry, prose, and creative writing are all forms of expressing yourself and your feelings. Writing down and acting out your thoughts can help to transform the intangibility of your emotions and experiences into something more tangible. They allow you to make your emotions tangible and real.

The ability to use language as a tool to help yourself and, more importantly, others. It properly allows me to express myself on a public platform for others to see. It allows me to visualize ideas that can be expanded upon in the future. It allows others to see those ideas and build on them as well. The tone captures the moment's emotion, while the word order and style represent the writer's stage of psychological development at the time of inscription. At the same time, the piece can reveal a lot about the writer's health and education level. Self-reflection is essential for developing empathy, maturity, morality, and philosophy.

Poetry and spoken word are powerful artistic expression mediums. They enable you to add tone and color to your writing. You don't have to be an artist or a performer to participate. You don't have to dazzle an audience or make them cry. You don't even have to expose your work to the public eye. However, the act of writing or speaking itself can be transformative. So don't worry if you want to try your hand at creative writing but don't know where to start. At first, no one does. Here are some writing prompts and poems to get you started. Please be aware that some of the languages in these poems are graphic or triggering when sexual assault.

Expressing with Woodcarving

Woodworking is classified as a "whole-brain activity." Some things that people do (such as recognizing faces) involve brain activity in a specific part of the brain or are only associated with one side of the brain. The general idea is that your right brain is more active with sensory inputs, emotions, and creativity, whereas your left brain is more active with number-crunching and logic. Consider (oh, there goes your left brain!) what happens in the woodworking industry. You must concentrate on visual work while also using hand-eye coordination and integrating senses such as sound, touch, and kinesthesia. When you work with wood, you use your entire brain; left, right, front, and back, as well as all the wiring in between. This is generally beneficial to mental health. Whole-brain activity tends to keep all of the neurological wiring functional, thereby preventing dementia.

A recent study investigated how "doing" art affects your brain differently than simply "seeing" art. The researchers divided the retirees into two groups: one group took a 10-week art appreciation class in a museum, and the other group took a 10-week art class where they created their artwork. The researchers then photographed (using functional MRI) which parts of the brain were active. They discovered that actively participating in the art generated more overall brain activity and connectedness than passively viewing art. They also discovered that changes in brain activity were directly related to improvements in "psychological resilience"—basically, your ability to deal with stress and adversity. This finding lends credence to the notion that a well-connected brain is healthier, contributing to a healthier person.

Creative activity not only keeps your brain healthy but can also help you deal with a variety of daily challenges. Art therapy has been used to treat chronic pain, traumatic brain injury, stress and anxiety problems, depression, and other mental disorders. For example, in Norfolk/Virginia Beach, a woodworking store runs a Woodworking for Veterans program to aid in the physical and emotional rehabilitation of wounded and injured military service members. According to research on art therapy, "art-based activities are of high benefit to psychological and social recovery, particularly in areas of self-discovery, self-expression, relationships, and social identity." Essentially, science is looking for creative activity.

DEAR ME...

Anxiety disorders frequently involve repeated episodes of intense anxiety, fear, or terror that peak within minutes (panic attacks). Anxiety and panic disrupt daily activities, are difficult to control, are out of proportion to the actual danger, and last long. You could avoid places or situations to avoid these feelings. Anxiety disorders properly include generalized anxiety disorder, specific phobias, social anxiety disorder, and separation anxiety disorder.

When to See a Doctor

See your doctor if:

- You have the impression that you are worrying excessively, interfering with your work, relationships, or other aspects of your life.
- You are bothered by and unable to control your fear, worry, or anxiety.
- You are depressed, have a problem with alcohol or drugs, or have other mental health issues in addition to anxiety.

- You believe your anxiety is related to a physical health issue.
- You have suicidal thoughts or behaviors; if this is the case, seek immediate emergency treatment.

Your concerns may not go away on their own, and if you do not seek help, they may worsen over time. Consult your doctor or a mental health professional before your anxiety worsens. If you seek treatment as soon as possible, it will be easier to treat.

While it is normal to be nervous before a big event or a big change in your life, approximately 40 million Americans suffer from an anxiety disorder, which is more than just the occasional worry or fear. Anxiety disorders could range from Generalized Anxiety Disorder (GAD), the intense worry that you can't control, to panic disorder, which is characterized by panic attacks, heart palpitations, trembling, shaking, or sweating.

It is critical for those suffering from an anxiety disorder to consider talk therapy or medication strategies that can help manage or reduce anxiety in the long run. However, everyone can benefit from reducing stress and anxiety through lifestyle changes such as eating a well-balanced diet, limiting alcohol and caffeine, and making time for themselves.

Furthermore, there are steps you can take as soon as anxiety begins to take hold. Try these expert-backed suggestions to help you relax your mind and regain control over your thoughts.

1. Stay in your time zone.

Anxiety is a forward-thinking state of mind. Ask yourself, "What's going on right now?" Is my life in danger? Is there anything I should do right now? If not, she suggests making an "appointment" with yourself later in the day to revisit your worries so that those distant scenarios don't throw you off track.

2. Relabel what's happening.

Panic attacks frequently make you feel as if you are dying or having a heart attack. "I have a panic attack, but it's harmless, it's only temporary, and there's nothing I need to do," Chansky says. Furthermore, keep in mind that it is the inverse of a sign of impending death: your body is activating its fight-or-flight response, the system that will keep you alive, she says.

3. Fact-check your thoughts.

According to Chansky, people who suffer from anxiety frequently focus on the worst-case scenario. To combat these fears, consider how realistic they are. For example, assume you're nervous about a big work presentation. Rather than saying, "I'm going to bomb," say, "I'm nervous, but I'm prepared." Developing a habit of rethinking your fears trains your brain to find a rational way to deal with your anxious thoughts.

4. Breathe in and out.

Deep breathing can help you relax. While you may have heard of specific breathing exercises, Chansky says you don't need to worry about counting your breaths. Instead, concentrate on evenly inhaling and exhaling. She claims that doing so will help you slow down and re-center your mind.

5. Follow the 3-3-3 rule.

Take a look around you and list three things you notice. Then, identify three sounds that you hear. Finally, make three different movements with different parts of your body: your ankle, fingers, and arm. According to Chansky, this mental trick can help center your mind and bring you back to the present moment whenever you feel your brain racing at 100 miles per hour.

6. Just do something.

Standing up, taking a walk, throwing away a piece of trash from your desk – any action that interrupts your train of thought can help you regain control, according to Chansky.

7. Stand up straight.

"When we are nervous, we bend over to protect our upper body, which contains our heart and lungs," Chansky adds. Pull your shoulders back, stand or sit with your feet apart, and open your chest as an immediate physical antidote to this natural reaction. This helps your body feel like it's back in control, she says.

8. Stay away from sugar.

When you're stressed, it's tempting to reach for something sweet, but that chocolate bar may do more harm than good, as research shows that eating too much sugar can worsen anxious feelings. So rather than reaching for the candy bowl, Chansky suggests drinking a glass of water or eating protein, which will provide your body with slow energy that it can use to recover.

9. Ask for a second opinion.

Chansky suggests calling or texting a friend or family member and discussing your concerns with them. "Explaining them to someone else can help you see them for what they are." It can also help to write down your fears.

10. Watch a funny video.

This final strategy may be the simplest of all: Play clips from your favorite comedian or TV show. Laughter, according to Chansky, is a good antidote to anxiety. According to research, laughter has numerous benefits for our mental health and well-being; one study discovered that humor could help lower anxiety as much as (or even more than) exercise. Although stress and anxiety can happen in the workplace and your personal life, there are many simple ways to deal with them. These suggestions frequently involve diverting your attention away from the source of your stress. In addition, exercise, mindfulness, music, and physical intimacy can help alleviate anxiety while also improving your overall work-life balance.

GET BUSY

People live busier lives these days, taking on more and more with each passing month more work commitments, relationship commitments, family commitments, social commitments, and the list goes on... As a result, staying happy and relatively balanced appears to be a Sisyphean task (the mythological man who rolled a boulder up a mountain every day only to have it roll back down at the end of the day), i.e., impossible.

Is it possible to be balanced and happy when you have a massive workload? Unfortunately, no. Don't get me wrong: it's a difficult tightrope act to master, but don't worry: plenty of people have devised their methods for accomplishing everything they need to do while also making time for everything else they want to do in life. This is the art of balancing one's life. Here are just seven of the best tips that I wholeheartedly recommend if you're struggling to find a way to maintain your balance while also being happy.

How to get busy with Exercise and activity

Read Zen Habits: Or whatever your preferred diversion is. Even better if it will help you live a better life. Simply limit the amount of time you read at one time, so you don't read through the Zen Habits archives in one sitting.

Declutter your workspace: If I don't have anything else to do, I'll clear off my desk (if there is anything there) or start looking around critically at everything in sight and asking myself, "Does that need to be there?" "How can I make this easier?" Strange, I know, but I have an unusually uncluttered workspace. My desk right now consists of a table, my iMac, and nothing else. There were no files, papers, or office supplies. Everything is done on my computer, which I enjoy. There is nothing on my walls. You may not require anything so austere, but decluttering can be a lot of fun.

Pursue a hobby: My hobby was blogging... I'd do it in my spare time at work or before or after work. Most can not pursue their hobby at work — model airplane glue may irritate your coworkers, but you can read about it on occasion. By the way, I was open about my blogging and freelancing at work with my boss, but many people get away with it on the side. I'm not going to be making any recommendations, but please do not be fired.

Make your work a game: Anything can be turned into a game. Determine how many widgets you can produce in 10 minutes. Assume your coworkers are evil villains. Assume you're a CIA agent in disguise, and no one knows. Or perhaps a fairy princess. Whatever makes you happy.

Educate yourself: On Guam, this is referred to as "education" — it's not a real word, but we like to play with words. You have the potential to be your college professor. Wikipedia is a fine place to begin, but you should branch out from there if you want to become an expert in anything.

Play Sudoku: Perhaps not the most intellectual or exciting game of all time. Of course, I only played it for a short time and did not become addicted like other people I know, but I must admit it is a fun way to pass the time.

Choose a soothing desktop picture: When I'm procrastinating, I like to do this. I'll go online and look through Flickr or some desktop wallpaper website until I find a very simple, soothing image. I probably do this once a month or so.

Do some pushups and crunches: If you are bored, you might as well start working out. You can do pushups and crunches right next to your desk (or go outside if you're concerned about your coworkers noticing). Or walk up some stairs, or do squats and lunges without weights, or chair dips, or whatever.

Drink some water: Dehydration can cause us to feel tired and sluggish. Water can revitalize us. Keep the water coming all day — you might need to pee more.

Read: I like to bring a book with me wherever I go. Then I pull it out whenever I have free time, whether I'm waiting at the doctor's office, in line at the post office, driving in the Indy 500, or whatever. If it's not a novel, keep a "to read" folder with things you want or need to read but don't have time for right now... Then, when you're bored at work, pull it out. You could also keep a "to read" folder on your computer.

Start writing your novel: Some of us have a novel circling in our heads and hearts, ready to be written. So, mister, get it out there. Begin by jotting down some ideas for characters, plot, and what the hell this book is about in the first place. It isn't going to come out on its own.

Take a nap: If you're not using a good place to sleep, you can sleep in your car or curl up with a sweater under your desk. I've figured out how to fall asleep in my chair, but luckily I work from home and can nap on the couch if I need to.

Create a new project: If things are getting stale at work, try something new. Innovate and create. What can you do to make a long-term difference for your company and yourself, for your career? If you're stuck in a rut, invent a new one for yourself. It makes no difference if it is not part of the job description. You may need to consult with your boss, but sometimes you can just get started and notify the higher-ups later. They'll be happy if it's good for the company and they're smart.

Write a love letter: If you have got a significant other, write them a letter in which you explain why you adore them. They'll adore it. Email is convenient, but pen and paper are preferable.

Do one small thing to increase your wealth: This could include opening a savings account if you don't already have one or setting up an automatic transfer from checking to savings every payday, researching a money market fund or index fund, or simply reading Get Rich Slowly for personal finance basics.

This is something I enjoy doing when things slow down. I'll just open a text file and start typing. Of course, I love lists (you should know that by now), so I'll often just start making a list and writing down my thoughts. If things move too slowly, I'll write the entire blog post. If necessary, I can always post it later. Make sure you're passionate about what you're writing about.

Do an errand: This can happen in the office ("Where is that ink cartridge I've been looking for all week?") or outside the office ("I need to buy toilet paper today!"). It gets you moving, takes you away from your boredom, and accomplishes something useful.

Update your finances: I used to track my finances with Microsoft Money, but now I use a Google spreadsheet online and accessible from anywhere. Other online solutions were considered, but I prefer to keep things as simple as possible. Regardless of how you do it, it's a good idea to update your financial tracking system once a week, so you know where you stand and don't overspend. Do you have some free time?

Meditate at your desk: Some might argue that this is just a fancy way of saying "take a nap." But the key for me is to close my eyes and concentrate on my breathing rather than falling asleep. This has nothing new-age about it; it simply brings your attention back to the present moment and calms you. But, on the other hand, it can sometimes relax you so much that you fall asleep. Two birds, one stone, I say.

How to keep your body busy to feel better physically

Organize your files: Many people may find this tedious, but I enjoy organizing things. I get a strange satisfaction from getting rid of useless items and making everything smaller, neater, and more organized. It doesn't take long either.

Get wild: Occasionally, we just have to let everything hang out. Begin singing or dancing at the top of your lungs around the office. People may stare or laugh, but having a little fun at work isn't a bad thing. Alternatively, get out of the office and do something exciting or outlandish. One afternoon of craziness won't hurt you (well, stay away from things that are illegal or life-threatening, if possible).

Crank up the tunes: Some upbeat music may do the trick. They can make any job more enjoyable. Play it through your speakers if your coworkers don't mind, or plug in your earbuds. Radiohead, Clap Your Hands Say Yeah, the Yeah Yeah Yeahs, Jack Johnson, Snow Patrol... are currently on my playlist. I could go on forever.

Clear out your inbox: I enjoy having an empty inbox, whether my email inbox or a physical one. Crush it until it's empty — you don't have to do everything in the inbox; just make a note of it on your to-do list if you intend to do it later (or delete, file, forward, or do it now). Have a thousand or two emails piling up in your inbox? Place them in a temporary folder and complete them later, beginning with a clean inbox. Most likely, you won't need to do them at all. Simply keep your inbox empty from now on.

Take a day or two off: Sometimes, all you need to do is take a break and recharge your batteries before getting back to work. While you're away, don't do any work. Instead, veg out, read, sleep, exercise, or do whatever you want. Take your attention away from your work. Consider your priorities. Get outside and enjoy nature. Reestablish contact with your life.

Take a walk: This is often all I require, especially if I've been sitting all day and my blood is pooling in my buttocks and legs. I need to get some blood flowing! So go outside, take a walk, observe people and nature, and reflect on your day, your life, and the people in it.

How to help influence the mental state

List your life goals: What do you hope to achieve in life? If you've previously listed them, it's always a good idea to update them. Then pick one of those goals to work on this year. Next, consider what you can do today to get closer to that goal, even if it's just a small step. Set things in motion. Do this every day to get closer to your goal.

Pursue your next job: If your job is so boring that you don't know what to do with yourself, it's time to find a new one.

Instead of quitting right away, start looking for your next job. Look for openings, make phone calls, update your resume, send it to a few places, fill out some applications, and send some email feelers. Find something that will never bore you and that you will be passionate about.

Create a new challenge: I believe this is by far the best item on the list, but you may disagree. So many times, we are bored because there is no challenge — things are too simple or routine. So, rather than waiting for someone to create a challenge for you, create one yourself. How can you push yourself? Set a new work goal. Set a goal for yourself to produce more than ever before. Investigate new projects. Set and pursue personal goals. Whatever piques your interest.

Improve your skills: Along the same lines, pick a skill that needs honing and set a goal for yourself to improve, whether it's computer programming, writing, or working with Adobe InDesign. Then, improve your skills — you can use them to advance your career, find a new job, or become self-employed. Or simply have the satisfaction of knowing you're the best at what you do.

ARE YOU TALKIN' TO ME?

Remain Connected with Other

It is critical for happiness and overall well-being to be surrounded by family and friends. According to research, strengthening your relationships can even help you live a longer life. Unfortunately, staying in touch with loved ones can be difficult, if not impossible, for those who live far away. Fortunately, there are numerous ways to hear, see, and communicate with those important to you, even if they are not physically present. Here are some ways to share fun and memorable experiences with family and friends worldwide, ranging from virtual happy hours to exploring outer space.

Start a remote book club

Starting a remote book club is a great way to connect with fellow book lovers and even discover a new author or genre. Organize a virtual gathering of family, friends, and others to discuss a book chosen by the group. Join an existing book club to meet people from all over the world. Rebel Book Club is a global organization with six locations that hosts monthly virtual book discussions. Do you need book suggestions? Check out the list of 50 popular Book Club Books on Goodreads.

Host a virtual game night

Host a virtual game night with family and friends to keep the traditional game night alive. Instead, organize a fun-filled evening to combat the distance blues and get your adrenaline pumping (with a little friendly competition, of course). Houseparty is a successful movie chat app that allows up to eight people to talk simultaneously and features games like Heads Up and Chips and Guac.

Travel the world together – virtually

Can't get away to see your significant other, family, or friends? Thanks to the internet, you and your loved ones can "travel" the world together without ever leaving your home. From your computer chair, you can explore the depths of the Paris Catacombs or Google Maps, where you can see everything from the Colosseum and the Palace of Versailles to the base camp of Mt. Everest.

Celebrate special occasions with a video

Do you need to be apart for a birthday, anniversary, or another significant event? Distance does not have to mean missing out on celebrations; you simply have to reinvent them. Send a personalized video of yourself along with a heartfelt message to that special someone. While it may not be as good as celebrating in person, the recipient will have the video message forever. Go the extra mile by organizing a group of family and friends to record a special video message for whoever you're celebrating. Be inventive! Put the video messages together, and your recipient will have a heartfelt, one-of-a-kind keepsake to treasure for years.

Go old school with snail mail

Although many of us long for the day when our inboxes will be empty, receiving a card or letter in the mail is always appreciated. Whether it's for a special occasion or simply to say "hello," don't underestimate the power of a card or letter.

Binge-watch your favorite shows together

It's fun to start a virtual book club with your loved ones, but there's nothing wrong with binge-watching your favorite shows with them as well. Distance, thankfully, does not have to be a barrier between you, your family and friends, and your favorite shows. Streaming services like Netflix Party make watching shows together across time zones easier with features like group chat and synchronized video playback.

Share recipes and cook together

Learning to cook together can be a great way for family and friends to bond, and fortunately, you can still gather in the kitchen virtually. To stay in touch, ask mom to teach you how to make your favorite childhood dish, host a cooking party, or start a "cook club." Each week, have the group choose a recipe that everyone will make. Next, get to work in the kitchen and schedule a virtual meeting to discuss your trials and tribulations. Are you looking for more kitchen ideas? Online food preparation classes and chef-hosted cooking demos on Instagram, such as Chef Jose Andres, can teach you and your family new skills for free.

Eat a meal together online

Food is a means of connection, so it's fortunate for us that you don't have to break bread with your family and friends because of distance. Set aside time to share a meal with your loved ones virtually. Join a FaceTime or a digital conference provider call and catch up over a meal. Do you wish to go all-in? Set your table, lay down a tablecloth, and pop a bottle of bubbly even when you're having dinner while they're having brunch.

Make a collaborative playlist

Spotify's collaborative playlist feature is ideal for sharing songs and mixing music genres to create a one-of-a-kind international playlist. Simply download the music streaming service, select "Collaborative Playlist," and copy the playlist link. Then, send the link properly to your family and friends so they can add music from their accounts.

Visit museums around the world together

There are thousands of world-class museums that provide virtual tours and online collections that you can explore from the comfort of your own home. Google Arts and Culture is a great resource for finding virtual tours from all over the world, and it's open 24 hours a day, seven days a week, so you can stay in touch with family and friends in any time zone. These virtual tours are completely free and range from the Museum of Modern Art in New York City to the Musée d'Orsay in Paris.

Phone a friend

Staying connected can sometimes be as simple as picking up the phone—and no, we don't mean texting. It is not uncommon in today's digitally-focused world for most of our communication to take the form of texting or social media. It is a tried and true way to keep in touch with family and friends. Most phones allow you to talk on multiple lines simultaneously, making it simple to communicate with a larger group. Send a greeting of "Good morning" or "Good night" to family and friends on the other side of the world.

Make the most of messaging apps

Aside from Facebook and Instagram, apps like WhatsApp can help you easily communicate with loved ones on the other side of the world. Send texts, pictures, videos, voice notes, or use group chats to bring the entire family together.

Take an online workout class

Working out with family and friends is an excellent way to motivate yourself to live a healthier lifestyle. Thanks to the internet, you can properly exercise with your loved ones even if they are on the other side of the world. If you Google "free online workouts," you'll get thousands of results for video workouts that will help you get your heart rate up at home. Make a workout date with your best friend and prepare to sweat.

Learn something new together

Learning something new with family or friends is a great way to strengthen your bond. There are numerous ways for you and your loved ones to learn together, thanks to MasterClass. Annie Leibovitz, a renowned photographer, will help you improve your photography skills. Judd Apatow, the comedic genius, teaches us how to get laughs. Alternatively, you could test your acting skills with none other than Samuel L. Jackson.

Place a different type of space between you

Looking for a fun way to stay in touch with family and friends when you're apart? Consider traveling to space. You and your loved ones can now tour the International Space Station together from the comfort of your own homes, thanks to NASA.

Have a good laugh with your friends. Laughter is beneficial to the soul, especially when it is shared. Set aside some time for you and your loved ones to connect via FaceTime, Google Hangouts, Skype, or Zoom and watch a stand-up comedy show online. Even if you can't be physically together, sharing a laugh can bring everyone together.

Value of Friends and family relations and professional help

Cherish and strengthen your ties with family

These are frequently our longest-lasting relationships, particularly with siblings. Concentrate on what keeps you together while respecting differences of opinion and worldview. Even if it's as simple as making pancakes on the weekend or going to a ballgame once a year, shared rituals help to keep families together. Try to have daily rituals (such as saying "I love you") with close family members and weekly, monthly, or annual rituals with those who live far away. Birthdays and holidays aren't the only occasions when you should call or send a card. Establish a time for quick check-ins. According to research, short, regular conversations keep you closer than longer ones at random intervals. People want three things in a friend throughout their lives: someone to talk to, rely on and enjoy themselves with.

When you are young, the time and effort you put into important relationships and friendships will pay off handsomely now and in the future. One study that followed college students for nearly 20 years discovered that the number of time friends invested in each other predicted whether they would remain close decades after graduation. Commitment to the relationship and effective communication were the keys to its long-term viability. Invest in your friends like you would a retirement fund by making regular "deposits" into your emotional account. Be there for them when they are going through a difficult time, such as when they are sick or feeling "down," and when they are celebrating a happy event, such as a birthday or a wedding.

A concert can be viewed from the comfort of your own home

Nothing beats seeing one of your favorite bands with your loved ones by your side. Many concerts, festivals, and other performances are streamed live for fans all over the world. Find a concert, festival, or performance that you enjoy and coordinate with family and friends to watch it from the comfort of your own home. NPR Music provides a list of live audio and streaming performances and links to streaming platforms such as Instagram and YouTube.

Get together for virtual happy hour

Even if you can't raise your glasses in person, you can still enjoy a drink with family and friends. Virtual happy hours are a fun way to connect with people in different time zones when distance impedes. FaceTime, Google Hangouts, Skype, and Zoom are excellent tools for sharing a few drinks with family and friends while keeping happy hour alive. Use a time that works for everyone, send a calendar invite, choose a signature drink, or share recipes for your favorite cocktail or mocktail. It's 5 p.m. somewhere in the world!

I'M TALKIN' TO ME (?)
How does Mediation work

Mediation is a process in which disputing parties attempt to reach an amicable settlement with the assistance of an impartial third party who mediates between them. The mediator leads the parties through a discussion process to help them reach an agreement at the end. Many people believe that mediation is a causal process in which a friendly mediator converses with the disputants until they abruptly drop their hostilities and collaborate for the common good. But unfortunately, this is not how it works.

Mediation is a multi-stage process that is intended to produce results. Although less formal than a trial or arbitration, the mediation process has distinct stages that account for the system's high success rate. The majority of mediations go as follows:

Mediator's opening statement: After the disputants have been seated at a table, the mediator introduces everyone, explains the mediation's goals and rules, and encourages each side to work cooperatively toward a resolution.

Disputants' opening statements: Also, every party is invited to describe the dispute and its financial and other implications. The mediator may also entertain general resolution ideas. The other person is not permitted to interrupt while the first is speaking.

Joint discussion: Depending on the participants' receptivity, the mediator may encourage the parties to respond directly to the opening statements to define the issues further.

Private caucuses: The private caucus allows each party to meet with the mediator privately. Each side will be housed in its room. The mediator will move between the two rooms to discuss each position's advantages and disadvantages and exchange offers. During the time allotted, the mediator will continue the exchange as needed. These private meetings are the heart of mediation.

Joint negotiation: After caucuses, the mediator may bring the parties together to negotiate directly, but this is unusual. Typically, the mediator does not bring the parties together until a settlement is reached or the mediation period expires.

Closure: Whereas if parties reach an agreement, the mediator will most likely put the main provisions in writing and request that each party signs a written agreement summary. Suppose the parties are unable to reach an agreement. In that case, the mediator will assist them in determining whether it would be beneficial to meet again later or continue negotiations over the phone.

Meditation vs. other forms of help for anxiety

Meditation has received a lot of positive press recently as researchers discover that it has a slew of brain benefits, including making us happier and stimulating the growth of brain regions responsible for memory formation, emotional regulation, and helping us gain perspective. However, can the practice help patients suffering from depression or anxiety and those taking antidepressants or anti-anxiety medications manage their symptoms? A meta-analysis of 47 clinical trials involving over 3,500 participants with mild anxiety or depression discovered that those who participated in mindfulness meditation classes experienced mood improvement after eight weeks, comparable to the effect seen with prescription medications. In addition, the study, published on January 6 in JAMA Internal Medicine, discovered that meditation helped relieve chronic pain in people suffering from back pain, arthritis, headaches, or other conditions.

"The benefits did fade over time, with meditation effectiveness decreasing by half three to six months after the training classes ended," said study leader Dr. Madhav Goyal, an assistant professor of medicine at Johns Hopkins University. The majority of the studies required volunteers to attend weekly two-hour classes to learn mindfulness meditation, which focuses on breathing, body sensations, and other present-moment experiences. Participants were also told to practice for 20 to 30 minutes every day at home. The meditating group was calculated according to the equation that attended health education classes about their specific health condition.

Meditation did not help with day-to-day issues like stress, sleep problems, or substance abuse. However, it also appeared to be as effective as other behavioral health strategies for assisting people with mood disorders and chronic pain, such as exercise, group therapy, and relaxation techniques. "Perhaps combining meditation with exercise or an antidepressant would be even more effective," Goyal speculated. "We'd like to investigate that further, but for the time being, we can advise anyone suffering from mild depression or anxiety to try a meditation program."

Many of Boston's higher education hospitals offer meditation classes to people suffering from various health issues that are exacerbated by stress. For example, nearly two decades ago, meditation guru Jon Kabat-Zinn established one of the country's first mindfulness meditation stress reduction programs at the University of Massachusetts Medical School in Worcester. The eight-week program at UMass Medical School consists of 212 hours of weekly classes that include meditation, yoga stretches, and group discussion. Students must also complete daily homework, such as meditating with instructional audio and attending a weekend meditation retreat. Depending on your income, the program costs between $475 and $630, not covered by insurance.

Massachusetts General Hospital teaches meditation and other relaxation techniques in its relaxation response resiliency program, which focuses on controlling the body's physiologic response to stress. Most insurance companies cover the first three appointments with a health care provider, but patients must pay $450 out of pocket for the eight weekly two-hour group sessions. A philanthropic grant has enabled cancer patients at Dana-Farber Cancer Institute to attend free meditation classes. "I see meditation as almost a requirement in any therapeutic regimen for cancer treatment, especially for patients who want a holistic approach to managing the illness," said Patricia Arcari, co-director of Dana-Farber Cancer Institute's Leonard P. Zakim Center for Integrative Therapies.

Patients anywhere at the stage of cancer treatment learn mindfulness techniques and the physical and emotional effects of stress in weekly 90-minute group classes held at Dana-Farber for eight weeks. "The meditation can help with pain management, nausea, and other side effects of treatment," Arcari explained, "but it also helps them express more self-compassion and appreciation for life." While Goyal and his colleagues did not find that meditation was associated with increased happiness or reduced stress, Arcari said she had seen anecdotal evidence of mood-lifting benefits in the two decades she taught meditation to patients. "I think meditation gives them a sense of calm, knowing they have some tools to deal with this difficult period in their lives," she said. "They can find some balance amid suffering."

Exploring other ways in which anxiety can be combated

When you're nervous or angry, you take quick, shallow breaths. According to Doherty, this sends a message to your brain, resulting in a positive feedback loop reinforcing your fight-or-flight response. That is why taking long, deep, calming breaths breaks the loop and allows you to relax. Next, allow yourself to express your anxiety or anger. When you label how you're feeling and allow yourself to express it, your anxiety and anger may subside. Several breathing techniques can help you relax. The first is three-part breathing. First, avoid physical activities that involve the expression of anger, such as punching walls or screaming. Second, close your eyes and visualize yourself calm after taking a few deep breaths. Finally, visualize your body relaxed, and imagine yourself navigating a stressful or anxiety-inducing situation by remaining calm and focused.

When you have a mental image of being calm, you can refer to it when you are anxious.

Let's clear up any misconceptions of meditation

Meditation has been hailed to improve mental health, alleviate chronic pain, reduce stress, and develop a new appreciation for our surroundings. Yet, even with all this interest, there are still misconceptions about what this ancient practice can do for human health and well-being.

Meditation is Just a Relaxation Technique

Relaxation is an important part of meditation, but vipassana-style meditation has a much higher goal. The same can be said for many other meditation systems. All meditation techniques emphasize mind concentration, bringing the mind to rest on one item or one area of thought. Jhana is the goal, and once attained, the experience is simply repeated for the rest of your life. This is not the case with vipassana meditation. Another goal of Vipassana is awareness. Concentration and relaxation are thought to be necessary companions to awareness. They are necessary precursors, useful tools, and advantageous byproducts. However, they are not the goal. The goal is to gain insight. Vipassana meditation is a profound religious practice that aims to purify and transform your daily life.

Meditation is Going Into a Trance

Again, the statement is correct for certain meditation systems but not for vipassana. Hypnosis is not a technique used in insight meditation. You are not attempting to black out your mind to become unconscious, nor are you attempting to transform yourself into an emotionless vegetable. The opposite is true: you will become increasingly sensitive to your emotional changes. You will come to understand yourself with greater clarity and precision. Certain states may appear trancelike to the observer while learning this technique. They are, however, the polar opposite. In a hypnotic trance, the subject is vulnerable to control by another party, whereas the meditator remains very much under their control in deep concentration. The resemblance is only superficial, and the occurrence of these phenomena is not the point of vipassana. As previously stated, Jhana is simply a tool or stepping stone on the path to heightened awareness. Vipassana is defined as the practice of cultivating mindfulness or awareness. According to the vipassana system's definition of the term, if you become unconscious during meditation, you are not meditating.

Meditation Is a Mysterious Practice That Is Impossible to Understand

Again, this is nearly true, but not quite. Meditation addresses levels of consciousness that go beyond conceptual thought. As a result, some of the experiences of meditation simply cannot be expressed in words. That is not to say that meditation cannot be understood. There are more profound ways to comprehend things than through the use of words. You are aware of how to walk. You probably won't be able to describe the precise order in which your nerve fibers and muscles contract during that process. But you already know how to do it. Meditation must be learned in the same way— by doing it. It is not something that can be learned in abstract terms, nor can it be discussed. Meditation is not a mindless formula that produces automatic and predictable results; you never know what will come up during any given session. Every time, it's an investigation, an experiment, and an adventure. This is so true that when you experience predictability and sameness in your practice, you can interpret it as a sign that you've gotten off track and are on the verge of stagnation. In vipassana meditation, it is critical to respect each second as the first and only second in the universe.

Meditation is used to develop psychic abilities

Meditation's goal is to raise one's level of awareness. It is not the goal to learn to read people's minds. The goal is not to levitate. The goal is to be free. There is a connection between psychic phenomena and meditation, but it is a complicated one. Such phenomena may or may not occur during the early stages of a meditator's career. Some people may have intuitive understandings or memories from previous lives, while others do not. In any case, these phenomena are not considered developed and reliable psychic abilities, and they should not be given undue weight. Such phenomena are quite dangerous for new meditators because they are quite seductive. They can be an ego trap, leading you astray. Your best bet is to avoid focusing on these phenomena. It's fine if they come up. If they don't, that's fine as well. At some point in the meditator's career, they may engage in special exercises to develop psychic abilities. However, this occurs much later in the process. Only once the meditator has advanced to a very deep stage of Jhana will they work with such powers without fear of being overpowered. The meditator will then cultivate them solely to serve others.

In most cases, this is only achieved after decades of practice. Don't be concerned. Simply concentrate on increasing your awareness. If voices or visions appear, simply acknowledge them and let them go. Do not become involved.

Meditation is risky, and a prudent person should avoid it

Everything is difficult. If you walk across the street, you might get hit by a bus. You could break your neck if you take a shower. When you meditate, you will almost certainly bring up a slew of unpleasant memories from your past.

Suppressed material that has been buried for a long time can be frightening. Exploring it, on the other hand, is extremely profitable. No activity is completely risk-free, but that doesn't mean we should wrap ourselves in a protective cocoon. That is not living; rather, it is death. Knowing roughly how much danger there is, where it is likely to be found, and how to deal with it when it arises is the best way to deal with it. That is the goal of this guide. Vipassana is the cultivation of awareness.

Meditation is for Saints and Sadhus

Of course, most holy men meditate, but they don't meditate just because they're holy. That is incorrect. And they began meditating before becoming holy; otherwise, they would not be holy. This is a critical point. A sizable number of students appear to believe that before beginning to meditate, one should be completely moral. It is an ineffective strategy. As a prerequisite, morality necessitates a certain level of mental control.

Meditation is Running Away from Reality

Meditation is a direct path into reality. However, it does not protect you from life's pain but rather allows you to delve so deeply into life and all of its facets that you break through the pain barrier and go beyond suffering.

Meditation is an excellent way to achieve euphoria

In a nutshell, yes and no. Meditation can sometimes produce lovely blissful feelings. However, they are not the goal, and they do not always occur. Furthermore, if you meditate with that goal in mind, they are less likely to occur than if you meditate solely for increased awareness. Bliss is the result of relaxation, and relaxation is the result of tension release. Seeking bliss through meditation introduces tension into the process, causing the entire chain of events to unravel. It's a Catch-22 situation: you can only experience bliss if you don't pursue it. Meditation is not intended to produce euphoria. It will occur frequently, but it should be regarded as a byproduct.

When you meditate, you sit in a circle and think lofty thoughts.

Of course, lofty ideas may emerge during your practice. They should not be avoided at all costs. They are also not to be sought. They are simply pleasant byproducts. Vipassana is a straightforward practice. It entails experiencing your life events directly, without preferences or mental images imposed on them. Vipassana is the practice of observing your life unfold from moment to moment without bias. What arises, arises. It is extremely simple.

After a few weeks of meditation, all of my problems will be gone

Sorry, but meditation is not a quick fix. You will notice changes right away, but the truly profound effects will take years. That is simply how the universe is built. Nothing worthwhile is accomplished in a single day. Meditation is difficult in some ways, requiring a long period of discipline and a sometimes painful practice process. Each sitting yields some results, but they are frequently subtle. They happen deep within the mind and only become apparent much later. And if you're constantly looking for huge, instantaneous changes, you'll miss the subtle ones entirely. You will become discouraged, give up, and swear that such changes will never happen. Patience is essential. Patience. If you only learn one thing from meditation, make it patient. Patience is required for any significant change.

Learning how to turn off the negative voice inside

In our heads, we all have a constant soundtrack of self-talk. It is stronger in some than others, and the content varies as well. Much of it is harmless, even helpful—"Don't forget, you're meeting with John"—but if your inner voice ever becomes negative, you must know how to control it. Here are some effective ways to silence your negative self-talk:

As if you were telling someone else, pay attention to what you're telling yourself: We would never speak to another person the way we speak to ourselves. We're far too often negative, condescending, or downright rude. Learn to properly treat yourself with the compassion, patience, and respect you would show to anyone else.

Remember, someone is listening: If you have positive self-talk, you will have positive thoughts and actions; if you have negative self-talk, you will have negative thoughts and actions—and, most likely, negative outcomes. Negative self-talk can even lower your self-esteem, so remind yourself that you're listening to yourself and that the consequences are just as real as they would be if you were talking to someone else.

Be mindful of what you say: Rethink your ideas. Sometimes just repeating a thought a few times and paying attention to what we're saying is enough to bring us back to reality. Work to develop a more constant conscious awareness of how you speak to yourself over time.

Stop judging yourself so harshly: A large part of low self-esteem stems from harsh and merciless self-judgment. Our judgment can be distorted at times, and our thoughts can become warped into negativity. If you have a habit of harshly judging yourself, the best way to curb your negative self-talk is to ask others how they see you and listen to what they say. You might be pleasantly surprised! Another technique is to imagine yourself in the shoes of someone with comparable talent, ability, and accomplishments.

Accept your imperfections: Nobody is perfect, and the sooner you realize this, the better off you'll be. We all have our own set of strengths and weaknesses. If you choose to focus on your flaws rather than your strengths, you will spend your entire life believing that you will never measure up. However, if you choose to spend your time doing what you excel at, your thoughts will be positive and gratifying.

Back up for a better view: Take a step back and listen to your thoughts if you're serious about taming your self-talk. Write them in any format that appeals to you in a journal, then go back and read them after some time has passed. Once you've done that, you're already in the repair process. When we create distance, we can sometimes see how far we've come.

Distract yourself properly to reboot your mind properly: You may become so preoccupied with overthinking everything that your thoughts circle in circles. Distract yourself if this occurs. Put your thoughts aside and get to work. Stop chasing after the wrong things and give yourself time to catch up with the right ones. Maybe by distracting yourself, you'll be able to figure out what's best for you.

Not everything true in the past is true today: Something that happened to you does not make it true today. You are more skilled and qualified to do what needs to be done in the here and now. Any thoughts and beliefs you had about yourself in the past no longer apply. Nevertheless, some things must be left in the past as we strive to succeed in the future. In short, there are only two things that can keep us from being positive and happy: living in the past and negatively treating ourselves. Don't be guilty of either; instead, learn to control your negative thoughts and focus on the future.

DO NOTHING

Doing nothing and thinking nothing makes you wise

How frequently do you do nothing? Nothing at all. Nothing like "just sitting on the couch and staring off into space, alone with your thoughts." Isolated from all distractions. If you're like the average person today, you're probably thinking "rarely" or, even worse, "never." We gladly charge our phones' batteries but neglect to change our own. When we are bored, we pick up our phones and scroll through social media, or we turn on the TV and binge-watch a show we've already seen. People are experiencing burnout at an all-time high because doing nothing has become obsolete.

You might be surprised to learn that doing nothing has some advantages. Turning off all distractions creates space for your subconscious to expand, resulting in increased creativity. When we are distracted, our minds tend to gravitate toward the most obvious solutions to solve problems. However, if you take the time to consider all of your options, you will come up with novel, inventive solutions that can lead to some life-changing ideas.

Boredom also alerts you when something isn't right. It's easy to ignore emotions and miss out on what your inner voice is trying to tell you when you're constantly buzzing around, checking off your to-do list. However, when you begin to quiet your mind and your surroundings, you may begin to feel those gut feelings rise to the surface, eventually motivating you to make changes that will improve your life.

Surprisingly, doing nothing can help you to be kinder. Being alone with our thoughts makes us yearn for a larger sense of purpose, prompting us to try new and challenging activities that extend beyond our own lives.

Even after reading about the numerous advantages of doing nothing, you may be thinking to yourself, "but I need to be productive at all times." This is particularly true for women. Sitting on the couch with dishes in the sink may seem strange, but this can be remedied with a mental shift. Instead of thinking of it as "not being productive," consider it an investment in your well-being. Because that is precisely what it is. You also don't have to cram an hour of anything into your schedule. Begin with five minutes each day at the same time. Don't worry if your thoughts wander to that email you forgot to send, or your breathing becomes labored. All of these reactions are normal and will pass. After a week or so, doing nothing will become a pleasurable experience. Yes, truly. So, today, do something nice for yourself: Don't do anything. It could be everything you're looking for.

We mean absolutely nothing when we say nothing. There will be no scrolling through social media, reading books or articles, listening to podcasts, or watching movies, TV shows, or YouTube videos. If you're like most Americans, you'll have to think about it because we don't do "nothing" very often. That isn't to say we aren't talking about the importance of work-life balance and meditation or extolling the virtues of relaxation — we are. Despite this trend, we are busier and more stressed than ever. Even when we are not working, many feel obligated to do something productive, whether going to the gym, running errands, attending a yoga class, or dealing with bills and other responsibilities. We feel obligated to squeeze productivity out of every last nanosecond of our daily lives, judging our worth as humans based on how successful we are in doing so.

Focus on Meditation

Focused meditation entails concentrating intently on staying in the present moment and slowing down the inner dialogue. Unlike traditional meditation, which involves focusing on nothing to quiet your mind, focused meditation involves remaining in the present moment while focusing entirely on one thing, typically sensory stimuli such as sounds, visual items, tactile sensations, tastes, smells, and even your breathing — similar to mindfulness meditation techniques.

Though you can begin practicing focused meditation in just five steps, this does not imply that each session will be easy, especially at first. Keep the following ideas properly in mind as you work to create a practice that is unique to your experience, environment, and enjoyment:

Give it time: Meditation frequently necessitates practice. If you expect to do it perfectly, you may end up causing yourself more stress. In addition, disappointment may prevent you from persevering. So, do nothing and concentrate solely on meditation.

Start with shorter sessions: For beginners, five minutes is sufficient. Then, gradually increase the length of your sessions.

Try another meditation practice: If the experience is frustrating and you don't want to continue, you might have better luck with other types of meditation, such as karate breathing meditation.

Choose the best time for you: Focused meditation (or any meditation practice) is a popular way to start their day. A morning meditation practice can help you stay calm and remind you to be mindful throughout the day. Others choose to meditate after work to unwind from their hectic schedules and refocus on their families and homes. Consider it a great way to leave work stress where it belongs — at work.

How doing nothing is hard... how to deal with that challenge

When confronted with unpleasant thoughts or feelings, the manic defense tends to distract the conscious mind with a flurry of activity or the opposite thoughts or feelings. The manic defense is exemplified by someone who spends all of his time rushing from one task to the next and cannot tolerate brief periods of inactivity. The expression on his face as he plows through yet another family outing, cultural event, or strenuous exercise routine reveals that his goal in life is not so much to live in the present moment as it is to cross items off his never-ending list. If you ask him how he is, he will most likely respond with an artificial smile and a robotic response along the lines of, "Fine, thank you—very busy, of course!" Yet, he is not fine in many cases but rather perplexed, exhausted, and deeply unhappy.

Other, more specific examples of the manic defense include the socialite who attends event after event, the small and dependent boy who charges around proclaiming that he is Superman, and the sexually inept adolescent who laughs "like a maniac" at the slightest hint of sex. It is critical to distinguish this type of 'manic laughter' from the more mature laughter that results from unexpectedly revealing or emphasizing the ridiculous aspects of an anxiety-provoking person, event, or situation. Such mature laughter allows a person to see a problem in a more accurate and less threatening context, thereby reducing the anxiety that it causes. All it takes to make someone laugh is to tell him the truth disguised as a joke or a tease; remove the disguise, however, and the effect is entirely different. In short, laughter can be used to either reveal or conceal or block out the truth, as in the case of the manic defense.

Indeed, the essence of the manic defense is to occupy the conscious mind with opposite feelings of euphoria, purposeful activity, and omnipotent control to prevent feelings of helplessness and despair from entering it. This is no doubt why people feel compelled not only to mark but also to celebrate such depressing milestones as entering the workforce (graduation), growing older (birthdays, New Year's), and, more recently, death and dying (Halloween)—laughing when they should cry and crying when they should laugh.

SEEING IS BELIEVING

Mindful meditation examples and anecdotes

Yawn and stretch for 20 seconds every hour. Make a fake yawn if necessary. This will set off genuine alarms. Say "ahh" as you exhale. Consider how a yawn affects your thoughts and feelings. This returns you to the present moment.

Then, stretch slowly for at least 10 seconds. Notice any tightness and say "ease" or simply "hello" to that location (being mindful — noticing without judgment). Take another 20 seconds to notice, then return to your previous task.

Three hugs, three big breaths exercise

Take three deep breaths together while hugging someone. Even if they wouldn't breathe with you, your breathing will ground them.

Stroke your hands

Reduce or close your eyes. Next, move your right hand's index finger up and down on the outside of your fingers slowly. After you've stroked your left hand mindfully, switch and let your left hand stroke the fingers of your right hand.

Mindfully eat a raisin

Consider eating a raisin or a piece of chocolate mindfully. Slow down, take everything in, savor it, and smile between bites. Slow down on purpose. Make use of all of your senses to see, touch, smell, and sense it. Then, gently place it in your mouth and savor it. Enjoy the texture, flavor, and feel of it in your mouth. Allow it to linger before swallowing. After you've swallowed it, raise your lips slightly and smile. Do the same thing with each raisin or bite you take.

Clench your fist and breathe into your fingers

Your fingers and thumbs should be facing down. Make a fist and clench it tightly. Turn your hand over so that your fingers and thumbs face up and breathe into your fist. Take note of what happens.

STOP

Stand up and take a deep breath. Feel your kinship with the earth.

Pay attention to your body. Reduce your gaze. Examine your body for physical sensations or emotions. On the out-breath, expel any unpleasant sensations, emotions, or feelings. Take note of any pleasant ones and allow them to fill you up on the in-breath.

Raise your head and properly take in your surroundings. Observe something pleasant in your surroundings and be grateful for it and its beauty.

Consider what is possible, what is novel, or what is a step forward.

If you find yourself being reactive, try the following steps:

Pause and take one to three big breaths.

Say "step back." (You don't have to step back physically, you can just do it in your mind.)

Say "clear head."

Say "calm body."

Breathe again. Say "relax," "melt," or "ease."

Mindful breathing for one minute

Lower your eyes and pay attention to where you feel your breath. That could be the flow of air through your nostrils or the rise and fall of your chest or stomach. If you can't feel anything, place your hand on your stomach and watch how it rises and falls gently with your breath. You can simply lengthen your in and out breaths or breathe naturally if you prefer. Your body understands how to breathe.

Loving-kindness meditation

Repeat for one minute: 'May I be happy, may I be well, may I be filled with kindness and peace.' You can substitute "you" for "I" and think of someone you know and like, or you can simply send love to everyone.

An aspiration

Choose an aspiration. Simply ask yourself, "What is my heart's aspiration?" Take a 20-second break. Repeat this process a second or third time, noting what happens. Perhaps it is to come from a place of love, be kind to oneself or others, or be patient.

How it helped others

Of course, when we meditate, it is not necessary to focus on the benefits but rather on the practice. There are numerous advantages. Here are the results of mindfulness practice.

Understand your pain: Pain is an unavoidable part of life, but it does not have to control you. Mindfulness can assist you in reshaping your relationship with both mental and physical pain.

Connect better: Have you ever found yourself staring blankly at a friend, lover, or child, unsure of what they're saying? Mindfulness allows you to give them your undivided attention.

Lower stress: There is a growing body of evidence that excessive stress causes or worsens various illnesses. Mindfulness reduces stress.

Focus your mind: It can be frustrating to have our minds wander and be pulled in six different directions. Meditation improves our natural ability to focus.

Reduce brain chatter: The droning, chattering voice in our heads never seems to leave us alone.

MAKE MY MIND MINE

How to be mindful

We are truly living in our heads. From day to day, we exist in a dream-like state in which we are neither connected to the world around us nor centered in our own body or being. Instead, we're preoccupied with memories, racing thoughts and worries about the future, and passing judgments and reactions to the few things we do see. So here are some simple methods to incorporate mindfulness into your daily life.

Observe your breathing

A single breath in and out, as Eckhart Tolle once said, is a meditation. Your breathing is both natural and rhythmic. When you pay attention to it, it transports you from your mind to your body. As a result, you are temporarily free of your racing thoughts, worries, and fears, and you are reminded of who you truly are — your inner spirit, not your thoughts.

Connect with your senses

Touch, smell, taste, sound, and sight are your portals into the present moment. However, when you are lost in thought, you are not aware of what your senses are picking up. So take a moment to enjoy the lovely aroma of your coffee. The salty sea breeze. The beauty and diversity of your neighborhood's flowers.

The tantalizing aroma of wood-fired pizza wafting from your neighborhood Italian restaurant as you pass by. Take note of how your clothing feels against your skin. In the morning, the soft clean bed sheets on your skin. The warm, comforting kiss of your lover. The grass beneath your feet. Put love and attention into your daily tasks, and you'll be surprised at how much joy and peace they can bring you.

Pause between action

Before answering the phone, pause and listen to the sound of it ringing.

Before starting your day's work, take a moment to feel the weight of your body in your chair.

Before you close your front door at the end of the day, take a moment to feel the handle. Adding mini-pauses between actions in your day can help you reconnect with your inner being, clear your mind, and recharge your batteries for the next task. Consider it as putting energetic bookends at the beginning and end of each activity.

Listen wholeheartedly

Most of us will never truly listen to people when they speak to us because we're too preoccupied with what we're going to say next, judging what they're saying, or getting completely lost in daydreams.

The next time you're in a conversation, make it your goal to fully listen to what the other person says without becoming distracted by your thoughts.

When it's your turn to speak, trust that you will intuitively know what to say next.

How mindful is different than meditation?

Although mindfulness and meditation are related, they are not the same thing. However, a basic understanding of the distinctions between these two concepts can assist you in establishing a practice that meets your needs.

There are numerous types of meditation, each with unique qualities and practices that guide the meditator in various directions of self-development. Therefore, choosing a meditation practice necessitates an understanding of one's goals and what each type of meditation offers.

Meditation is a Practice

To begin this investigation, it is helpful to review some definitions for the two constructs. First, one of the most popular Western writers on the subject and the creator of the Mindfulness-Based Stress Reduction program (MBSR), John Kabat-Zinn (1994), defines mindfulness as "the awareness that arises through paying attention, on purpose, in the present moment, non-judgmentally."

Contrast this with one researcher's definition of meditation: "Meditation is a practice in which an individual uses a technique – such as mindfulness or focusing the mind on a specific object, thought, or activity – to train attention and awareness and achieve a mentally clear, emotionally calm, and stable state."

Meditation is one of several paths to mindful living

One method for learning to live mindfully is through meditation. Meditation can also be viewed as a tool for cultivating mindfulness.

Meditation is extremely effective in helping people become more mindful in their daily lives. Those who practice mindfulness meditation in a systematic and disciplined manner, such as those who participate in the MBSR program, are more able to act mindfully in their daily lives (Carmody & Baer, 2008).

Although meditation is extremely effective for this purpose, it is only one of several methods for cultivating mindfulness, as we will see later.

Mindfulness can be used in the treatment that does not include meditation

Mindfulness is associated with numerous mental health benefits and other positive characteristics such as self-esteem and self-acceptance (Thompson & Waltz, 2007).

As a result of these factors, many practitioners regard mindful living as a worthwhile goal for their clients.

However, not all clients are open to meditation or willing to incorporate a formal practice into their daily lives.

Dialectical Behavior Therapy (DBT) is a great example of a treatment that uses mindfulness to help clients without requiring them to meditate in any formal way. Instead, DBT interventions are designed to assist clients in developing a "wise mind" by teaching them various skills that allow them to embody the qualities described by Kabat-Zinn.

Mindfulness can be practiced formally and informally

Meditation is a paradoxical practice because it is an exercise in "non-doing." In general, the task is to become an observer of one's inner world while exerting minimal effort and adopting a non-judgmental attitude.

These characteristics are opposed to how many of us live our lives: striving for advancement and prioritizing work over rest. Formal meditation, which involves sitting for a set amount of time, can provide a respite from the world's busyness and remind us that we don't have to work so hard to achieve our goals or be who we want to be.

Despite its many benefits, not everyone is interested in engaging informal mindfulness practice. These people may, however, want to be more mindful in their daily lives.

Mindfulness is only one aspect of meditation

Mindfulness is an important part of meditation practice, but other factors distinguish meditation. Concentration is another important aspect of meditation. When the mind is deprived of external stimuli, such as formal meditation, it is bound to wander to a thousand unexpected places. When the mind wanders, it is difficult to stay focused on the meditation practice at hand.

Training one's attention to concentrate more fully allows for more successful and fulfilling meditation, as well as possibly more mindfulness in one's daily life.

HOW TO MAKE THE WORLD DISAPPEAR

How to meditate

What we're looking for here is awareness, not some miraculous procedure that clears your mind of the myriad and unending ideas that erupt and ping in our brains all the time. We're merely practicing returning our focus to our breath when we sense it has wandered. Prepare to sit motionless for a few minutes by making yourself at ease. After you've finished reading this, you'll only focus on your natural breathing and expelling of air. Pay attention to your breathing. What's going on in your stomach? What's the deal with your nose? Keep your attention properly on your inhale and exhale. Inhale deeply, extending your belly, and then exhale gently, elongating the out-breath as your belly contracts. If you've encountered these sorts of distractions, you've discovered something important: they're the polar opposite of mindfulness. It's when we live in our minds, on autopilot, allowing our thoughts to roam here and there, investigating the future or the past, and so not being present in the now. But, to be honest, that's where the majority of us spend the majority of our time—and, to be honest, rather uncomfortable, if we're honest. This, however, does not have to be the case.

We "practice" mindfulness so that we may learn to notice when our brains are engaging in their regular everyday gymnastics and, if necessary, take a little break from them so that we can select what we want to focus on. In a nutshell, meditation helps us cultivate a far healthier connection with ourselves.

Practical solutions, not philosophies

Meditation is the process of directing one's entire attention to oneself by controlling one's breathing. Some may find it absurd to hear that to meditate, and one must control one's breathing. However, it is true that during meditation, one must control one's breath. This breath control does not imply that one must stop breathing. It is about paying close attention to every inhales and exhales. It is about deeply feeling every breath.

Though breathing control is the most important aspect of meditation, it requires a proper process. In response to whether meditation can be learned, we would like to inform you that meditation is a process that requires a great deal of patience. One cannot develop such patience independently, so one must learn meditation from a trained practitioner.

Meditation is something that anyone can learn. Everyone is capable of meditating, but it takes a strong will to do so. Therefore, before beginning to practice meditation, a person should be completely committed to it.

Meditation is not difficult to master. However, to achieve a state of calm in meditation, one must be extremely patient. It is because, at first, it may be difficult to concentrate, and one's mind may be filled with a plethora of nonsense thoughts.

THE MIND NEVER STOPS GROWING

Keep up the growth of the brain

The logical component of a teen's brain is still developing and will not be fully formed until around the age of 25. Recent research has discovered that adult and adolescent brains function differently. Adults think with the prefrontal cortex, the rational part of the brain. For many years, scientists assumed that as we age, hippocampal neurons cease to be generated. A new study, however, completely debunks this long-held belief. According to a new study, Pin it to Pinterest, and brain cells thrive even in older adults. During development, the brain grows at an astounding rate. Two hundred fifty thousand neurons are added every minute during brain development! The brain continues to grow for a few years after birth, and by the age of two, the brain is roughly 80% of adult size.

Meditation is not something to be mastered, and it's a continued evolution

There is a vast connection to the very source of who we are in the underbelly of our hearts and beings. If you've never been there, this may all sound Greek to you. But, as a Greek who has been meditating for years can attest, it is life-changing, life-enhancing — and the greatest secret to happiness, creativity, and calm. As a reason, there is no better time than the present to take advantage of this most sacred gift that has been freely given to us. To become a successful meditator, you should follow the following advice:

1. Always begin your practice with a heartfelt expression of gratitude. Consider a place that you enjoy and that brings you peace — and then transport yourself there in your creative imagination.
2. Concentrate on your heartbeat. This magical organ keeps you alive by pumping blood throughout your body. And be grateful for this miracle, as well as for every breath you take.

3. Take note of how your breath rises and falls. Be awestruck by your breath. Spend at least five minutes a day focusing solely on your breathing.
4. Consider each conscious breath as a bridge to the "you" who is wise, calm, and centered — and who knows you in your essence.
5. Put all judgments about your practice on hold. There is no wrong way to meditate; it is simply at one with yourself, wherever that may be.
6. Don't try to control your thoughts. It's like attempting to control a 500-pound gorilla. Allow your ideas and sensations to flow instead. Keep a watch on them for a while, then let them go. Simply, you don't relate to them. If your thoughts are racing, have a pen, and a notepad close by and scribble down what is upsetting you. It's another method for releasing pent-up emotions. Then return to your practice.
7. Consider how incredible it is that you have 37.2 trillion cells in your body right now that are producing, renewing, and keeping you alive. Reconnect with your gratitude now, just as you did

when you first started your practice. The operative term in meditation practice is simply that: practice!

Explore philosophical nature to help inspire the reader into action

Getting into a mindfulness meditation routine can be difficult if you lead a hectic lifestyle and constantly go. However, regular practice can benefit your busy lifestyle by making you more focused and capable of dealing with stresses that come your way. You may also notice that your meditation practice has given you greater energy.

Overcome difficulties keeping you from meditation

Quite often, you are unable to meditate regularly due to a specific problem or difficulty. If you didn't have a problem with meditating, you'd be doing it all the time! Consider what you genuinely want out of life above everything else. If you look closely, you'll notice that meditation provides a path to your deepest desires, such as peace, clarity, or happiness.

Schedule meditation

It's easy to forget to meditate, especially if you lead a busy life. Try this: make an appointment with yourself, just like you would a meeting or a doctor's appointment. Seeing the reminder can serve as a motivator to engage in some mindfulness practice. Because they use their diaries so frequently, many business people appreciate this tip.

Make a list of the benefits of meditation

Making a list of all the benefits of practicing mindfulness meditation regularly can help motivate you to keep it up.

Create a mindful space at home

Having a quiet, relaxing space in your home where you can meditate can be very motivating. So find a cozy corner in your home for soft cushions or beanbags, incense sticks, and whatever else makes you feel comfortable and relaxed to use as a meditation space if you have the space.

If you make a corner of your home appealing in this way, just seeing it may entice you to meditate. And, if you regularly practice meditation there, simply looking at or imagining yourself in that location can put your mind in a more meditative state.

Find a group or community to meditate with

Meditating with a team of like-minded people is highly effective and may tremendously inspire you to meditate regularly. If you can find a group or a community near you that you can attend a couple of times a week, you will be much more likely to stick to your meditation practice.

Look for a mindfulness or meditation group near you on the internet. Look for groups on Meetup, a website that connects groups of people with similar interests.

Make meditation a habit

You have a daily routine of waking up, washing your face, and brushing your teeth. Because you do it so frequently, you don't even think about it; your morning routine has become a habit. Incorporate your mindfulness practice in this way if possible. It should be as natural as brushing your teeth in the morning and evening.

Making a meditation session for the next day is the greatest method to build the habit of awareness. Then, on an actual day, you make certain that you complete the practice at the appointed time.

You'll be in the practice habit if you can instill a sense of determination within yourself and do this for about three weeks. Then you'll miss it if you skip the meditation! Meditating has become an essential part of your daily routine.

Deal with emotions that keep you from meditating

During meditation, upsetting and uncomfortable emotions and thoughts may arise. This situation makes it more difficult to stay motivated to meditate. Mindfulness is about accepting and listening to these emotions rather than trying to get rid of them. If you don't think you're ready to deal with it yet, talk to a counselor, a support group, or even your friends. Then, when you're ready, return to your mindfulness practice.

Eliminate distractions from meditation

Meditating becomes difficult when too many distractions surround you. Locate a quiet area away from the TV and computer, unplug the phone, and turn off your phone. If necessary, remove the batteries from the doorbell. Make sure you have your meditation time with as few interruptions as possible.

Practice meditation with music

If you find it too quiet on your own, you can listen to music while meditating. Find some soothing music to play over the guided meditations that come with this book. Your entire meditation can even consist of just listening to music mindfully. For wonderful calming effects, listen to soothing classical music on the radio or a CD.

Change posture during meditation

If sitting cross-legged during meditation makes you feel particularly uneasy, don't do it. Instead, choose a position that is a good fit for you. For your first few experiences with the practice, don't expect to be a seasoned Zen Buddhist monk sitting in the lotus position for hours on end. That can be discouraging!

If you need to lie down, go ahead and do so. If you feel very uneasy during the practice and want to move, do so. Remember that your practice is unique to you.

By finding a posture that feels right for you, you'll be more likely to enjoy and benefit from the practice. In addition, this result can serve as positive reinforcement for you, encouraging you to practice even more.

Printed in Great Britain
by Amazon